Contents

Seven—Exercises

Practical Criticism

John O'Neill, M.A. (Hons.)
Principal Teacher of English,
St. Mungo's Academy, Glasgow.

Robert Gibson & Sons, Glasgow, Ltd.
2 West Regent Street, Glasgow, C.2.

Acknowledgements

We value highly the permission to include copyright material and are happy to put on record our indebtedness for the following:

' Lecture Notes ' from *Spillout* by John Pudney, to the author and J. M. Dent and Sons Ltd.

' The Visitors ' from *The Storms* Poems by Peter Dale, to the author and Macmillan and Co. Ltd.

' The Folk Singers ' and ' Mid-Term Break ' from *Death of a Naturalist* by Seamus Heaney, to the author and Faber and Faber Ltd.

' The Planster's Vision ' from *Collected Poems* by John Betjeman, to the author and John Murray (Publishers) Ltd.

' A Poem about Poems about Vietnam ' from *Root and Branch* by Jon Stallworthy, to the author and Chatto and Windus Ltd.

' No ' from *Not that he Brought Flowers* by R. S. Thomas, to the author and Rupert Hart-Davis Ltd.

' Homage to a Government ' by P. A. Larkin, M.A., to the author.

' After the Wake ' by James E. McCormack, to the author (whom we have been unable to trace).

Printed in Great Britain
by Hay Nisbet & Co. Ltd.
© J. O'Neill 1969
SBN 7169 4066 3

Foreword

With the introduction of a new syllabus and a new examination in Higher English in the Scottish Certificate of Education, there is a need for some guidance on the question—at present optional—on Practical Criticism. This is new territory for most candidates, and indeed for many teachers. As a result, there is a possibility that many will 'play safe' and concentrate on the more traditional forms of question. This may not be a wise thing to do. In the past, the Literature section of the Higher paper has been the most poorly done, and the new paper is designed to encourage genuine responses to literature rather than re-statements, imperfectly learned, of other people's opinions. The question on Practical Criticism affords an opportunity to all candidates, even the mediocre, to score high marks in this one question—provided that they have had some training in what is required.

This book is not intended to be a teaching book, with exercises at every step of the way to test the pupil's grasp of what has been taught. It is, in fact, intended as a 'Do-it-yourself' book for all Higher English candidates, chiefly those from Further Education Centres and those who enter privately, but it is hoped that it will also be of some value to teachers and pupils in schools. It is pitched at the level of Higher English, but the basic principles described are equally applicable to English 'A' Level examinations, Scottish Certificate of Sixth Year Studies examinations, and even to the early stages of University examinations. The exercises included at the end of the book contain a series of questions on each poem, because this is the practice in Scottish examinations. But candidates for G.C.E. examinations, in which there are no set questions beyond a demand for a 'critical appreciation' of a poem, will find that the method suggested is adequate for their purposes.

No claims are made to originality of method or depth of observation. The book is merely a re-statement, in easily-understood form, of principles which have been known for many years—since in fact the term 'Practical

Criticism' was first introduced—though there is perhaps slightly more emphasis placed on grammar than is usually the case. What is claimed, however, is that the book is entirely practical, based on many years' experience of training candidates at this level.

Some care has been taken throughout—with occasional exceptions—to use in illustration, poems which will be familiar to most candidates for Higher English examinations. Almost all of the poems referred to can be found in the following books:—

The New Poetry (Penguin)
The Penguin Book of Contemporary Verse (Penguin)
Ten Twentieth Century Poets (Harrap)
The Golden Treasury (Oxford—1965 edition)

1   Introduction

Many people, especially students in examinations, when they are asked for an appreciation of a piece of literature, are guilty of at least one of two common faults. In the first place, they may give a purely *subjective* impression of what it conveys to them or how they react to it, without supporting their impression by a detailed consideration of what the author has said. On the other hand, they may provide a set of comments which they do not genuinely believe, but which they think are the 'correct' comments to make—again without close reference to the text to support what they say.

Practical Criticism is a method of close examination of a text in order to arrive at an appreciation of what the writer has said, which will be both *objective* and *independent*—that is, every comment will be based on the text, and every comment will be an expression of what the student has personally taken from it. It is a method which can be applied to all forms of literature, but in this book only the Practical Criticism of poetry will be considered.

A poet sets out to communicate some human experience—not necessarily his own—and the emotions and attitudes that accompany that experience. Since these emotions and attitudes are almost certainly very complex —otherwise it is unlikely that they would give rise to a poem of any merit—and since poetry is a very compressed form of communication, it is unlikely that any reader will immediately have a full understanding of what the poet has said. As he reads, he will be aware of the meaning in general terms, but full understanding will come only after considerable effort. Practical Criticism is an attempt to arrive at that full understanding, not just of meaning in the narrow sense but of all the devices by which the total meaning is conveyed by the poet and the poem makes its total impact on the reader. It is concerned with many things—word order, grammar, choice of words, sound effects, and so on—and especially it is concerned with those occasions when the poem departs from what might be considered the normal patterns of language.

This book will attempt to show how these various devices may be noticed and their significance evaluated.

WHAT KIND OF POEM?

This book is written with the requirements of the Scottish Higher Grade English examination specifically in mind, though its principles are not confined to that examination. Accordingly, the kind of poem discussed will be the kind of poem to be expected in Higher English, though it must be emphasised again that the principles of Practical Criticism can be applied to any form of literature.

The poem chosen will be generally modern, and probably not well known, though it may be by a well-known author. This is to avoid the danger of giving an advantage to students who have already studied the poem. It will always be fairly short and complete in itself, and the author's name will be stated. It will not contain anything which demands any specialised knowledge not likely to be possessed by all candidates, since this too would give an unfair advantage to some. The poem will not necessarily be a great masterpiece, but it will not be a bad poem deliberately chosen to catch out the unwary. It will always have some genuine experience to communicate in poetic terms, though this does not mean that everyone will be expected to like it.

In the course of the book, illustrations will be drawn from poems which do not conform exactly to this pattern, but the sample poems and questions at the end will all be of the kind to be expected in Higher English.

WHAT KIND OF QUESTIONS?

In English examinations in Scotland, both Higher and Sixth Year Studies, candidates are never presented with a poem and simply told to 'appreciate' or 'criticise' it. They can expect to be asked a few questions which are designed to lead them towards the essential meaning of the poem and towards particular parts which demand very close attention. The questions will not be simple questions of 'Interpretation' as in a Language paper, with answers which are 'right' or 'wrong'. They will always be open-ended questions, which can be dealt with either superficially or to a depth which will vary in direct proportion to the candidate's sensitivity to language and to the emotions it communicates. Always they will direct attention to the words of the text, either explicitly or implicitly. If candidates are asked for their reaction to the attitude expressed in the poem, it will only be after they have been directed towards close study of items of particular significance.

The nature of the questions, however, is unimportant at this point. What is necessary is that the student should become aware of what he ought to be looking for in poetic technique, so that in time he will become capable of a 'critical appreciation' even without the benefit of helpful questions. The principles he acquires in the course of his study should be applied to all of his reading of poetry, not just to the examination in Practical Criticism, and if this is done the examination questions should present no difficulty.

METHOD OF APPROACH

(1) Regardless of whatever questions may be asked about it, the first step in approaching a poem is obviously to read the whole poem thoroughly. Probably several readings of the whole poem will be required in order to find out what kind of poem it is, what it is generally about. At this stage the reader's response will be almost one of intuition, though he may notice a few points of technique which help towards understanding.

(2) This general impression of what the poem is about must then be related to the actual words of the text in order to arrive at the total meaning of the poem and to evaluate the author's technique.

(3) Finally, the reader must decide his personal reaction to what he has read.

This book will be concerned only with the second of these points, the close examination of the actual text of the poem.

Although they are closely interrelated, it is possible to isolate five different items which must be considered:—

Situation
Grammar
Choice of words
Sound patterns
Visual patterns

Each of these five items will be dealt with separately in the succeeding parts of the book.

2 Situation

In this section we shall be concerned with the relationship that exists between the poet and his audience, and the extent to which the language used is appropriate to that relationship. It will be convenient at this stage to explain two terms which will be useful at later stages—'register' and 'persona'.

REGISTER

'Register' is a very useful term which has been introduced in recent years by experts in the study of language. These experts recognise that the form of language we use is dictated by the situation in which we use it. Thus, for example, the language a man uses in writing a letter to a friend is different, both in grammar and vocabulary, from the language the same man uses in conversation even with the same friend. Even his conversational language will vary according to the person he is addressing. For example, he may bid good morning at various times to his wife, his children, his colleagues and his employer, but in each case the form of words will vary to some extent, and the greeting he gives his children will not be acceptable as a greeting to his employer. The minister of religion, acting in his capacity as minister, may address his Maker in the words,

"O God, our Father, grant that we thy children may at all times enjoy health of soul and health of body.",

but in his capacity as husband he would never say,

"O Jean, my wife, grant that we thy family may be fed this day with chicken and potatoes."

The scientist never boils water—water is heated to boiling point—except when he is behaving not as a scientist but as a man, in which case he simply boils the kettle like the rest of us. The politician in his public statements steers a course, guides the ship of state, tightens his belt, doles out equal slices of cake to all, and always keeps his hand on the nation's purse strings, but in his private conversation he probably uses no more metaphors than any other person. The professional author writing a story will expertly vary his sentences, using a well-balanced mixture of simple, compound , and complex sentences, yet the same man telling a story in private life to a circle of friends—even of fellow authors—will only rarely use subordinate clauses, will often begin his sentences with 'And', and will utter some sentences which would be quite unrecognisable as sentences if they were set down on paper. We can all recognise situations in which ignorance of the answer to a question posed might be expressed by:

I'm stumped.

I don't know.

I do not know.

I am unable to arrive at any solution to the problem. None of these sentences is 'right' or 'wrong', none of them is 'good English' or 'bad English', but they are not equally appropriate for a given situation. The competent user of English is the one who always selects instinctively which form of words is the form appropriate to the situation.

'Register' is the term applied to any particular form of language appropriate to a given situation. Register takes account of the person who makes the utterance, the person who receives the utterance, the relationship between them, and the situation in which the utterance is made. Those features of language which are characteristic of one register are known as 'markers'. Thus the passive voice can be a marker of the scientific register; the vocative case preceded by 'O' may be a marker of the register of prayer; contractions such as 'couldn't' and 'don't' may be markers of conversational language; a succession of simple sentences, many beginning with 'and', may be markers of the register of oral story-telling, particularly among children; the use of 'we' to denote 'I' is an indication of majesty, real or assumed; the same 'we' used to denote not 'I' but 'you' may be a marker of the register of medical consultation—"How are we today, Mrs. Brown?"

Very many broad categories of register can be identified in this way, and markers for each can be recognised.

There is, however, no finite list. The different registers are limitless in number, and the markers for one register may serve also as markers for several different registers. Nevertheless, as a broad classification, the term 'register' can be a very useful one.

Poets do not always speak as themselves. Sometimes they adopt the identity of some other person, real or imaginary, in a particular situation, also real or imaginary. Thus Robert Browning is not present in his poem 'My Last Duchess'. The poem is to be imagined as being the words of an ancient Italian nobleman talking to an emissary from the father of his prospective bride, and revealing unintentionally in his talk about his former wife exactly what kind of man he is. Similarly, the 'I' of 'The Love Song of J. Alfred Prufrock' is not T. S. Eliot, but Prufrock himself. The poet's function in such poems is to present the man and the situation as seen through that man's eyes, the poet's own attitude emerging only implicitly rather than explicitly. Whenever a poet uses this device, he is said to be adopting a persona.

Often, of course, the poet speaks as himself. Thus when Wordsworth says,

"I wandered lonely as a cloud
That floats on high o'er vales and hills,"

he is referring to himself and not to a persona adopted for the occasion.

QUESTIONS WE SHOULD ASK

In examining a poem, we must first of all identify the situation by answering certain questions.

Who is speaking? Is it the poet himself, or has he adopted a persona?

Who is receiving his words? Is he addressing us as readers of poetry, or is there some other person addressed, with ourselves merely eavesdroppers?

What relationship exists between speaker and audience?

C

What register has the poet adopted? What markers of that register can be noticed?

Is the register entirely appropriate for the situation? Has the register been maintained throughout, or has it been dropped—intentionally or otherwise?

If one of the tests of good poetry is its appropriateness to its situation, then asking and answering questions such as these should be the first task in considering any poem. In this way, Browning's 'My Last Duchess' will be seen to be a perfect expression of its situation. The persona is clearly brought out in the condescending politeness of the aristocrat to someone slightly inferior socially but nevertheless of sufficient rank to be engaged on a piece of delicate negotiation with him; the shrewd man of business revealed in his reference to the financial discussions just concluded; the connoisseur, with his pride in the possession of things of priceless value; the sheer arrogance of the man who 'chooses never to stoop'. In all these aspects the language can be seen to be entirely right for the occasion. Thus a consideration of situation can lead to a good general understanding of what the whole poem is about.

Similarly, in T. S. Eliot's 'The Love Song of J. Alfred Prufrock', the language reveals a lonely man tortured by uncertainty and self criticism, aware of the emptiness of the life around him, yet too timidly aware of his own shortcomings to take any decisive steps to remedy things. This by no means gives a full explanation of the poem, but at least, having recognised the situation, the reader can go on to search for all that the poem has to say about the situation.

In the third poem already referred to, 'The Daffodils', Wordsworth is clearly speaking as himself to his readers, with no intermediaries. He is setting out to recount an experience which he has had of the staggering beauty of nature, and to convey his discovery of how significant this experience has been to him since the event. All this he seeks to convey in simple everyday language which, despite its simplicity, brings out the living quality in what we might think of as inanimate nature. Once again, the register is entirely appropriate to the situation.

(1) "Now all you young fellows, take a warning from me,
And don't go a-courting every wee girl you see.
Don't look in her basket as she passes by,
Or she'll make you the daddy of wee Mind-Your-
Eye, laddie,
Fol de rol di, laddie, fol de rol day."

This is the ending of a humorous folk-song about a young man who chivalrously offered to hold a girl's basket while she "stepped round the corner some things for to buy", and was left literally holding the baby.

The singer is directly addressing his audience on a social occasion, and his aim is to amuse them, to involve them in a mock-serious way with his 'warning', and to get them to respond by joining in the last line, which is repeated at the end of each verse. The language chosen is entirely right for this situation—the direct address to the 'young fellows'; the use of everyday language and popular words such as 'wee'; the use of 'don't' and 'she'll'; 'daddy', instead of 'father', being used in conjunction with 'laddie'; the conversational 'now' at the beginning; the absence of complex sentence structures; the easily-remembered refrain. It is not great poetry, but it is certainly right for its situation.

(2) "As fair art thou, my bonny lass,
So deep in love am I;
And I will love thee still, my dear,
Till a' the seas gang dry."*

This time the poet is directly addressing one person, whom he wishes to impress with the depth and constancy of his love. The simplicity of the vocabulary is a mark of its sincerity, especially since it is set in dialect, and though his final assertion pitches things strongly it is a forceful and acceptable statement of his integrity.

(3) "This is the lower sling swivel. And this
Is the upper sling swivel, whose use you will see,
When you are given your slings. And this is the
piling swivel,
Which in your case you have not got. The branches
Hold in the gardens their silent, eloquent gestures,
Which in our case we have not got."†

15

* "My Love is like a Red Red Rose" (Robert Burns)
† "Naming of Parts" (Henry Reed)

Here two different registers are used. At first we have the voice of the instructor identifying to war-time army recruits, in well-rehearsed words, the parts of the rifle. At the end we have the unspoken and unmilitary thoughts of the poet, who is a soldier in nothing but the uniform he wears. These contrasting registers are maintained throughout the five stanzas of the poem, making an eloquent comment—not stated explicitly by the poet—on the lack of sensitivity that is bred by war.

(4) "Once I am sure there's nothing going on
I step inside, letting the door thud shut.
Another church: matting, seats, and stone,
And little books; sprawlings of flowers, cut
For Sunday, brownish now; some brass and stuff
Up at the holy end; the small neat organ;
And a tense, musty, unignorable silence,
Brewed God knows how long. Hatless, I take off
My cycle-clips in awkward reverence.*

Here we have the poet speaking in his own person to us as his familiars, conveying what is a problem to many people in contemporary society—his rejection of what the Church stands for, and yet his awareness that with its passing an uncomfortable gap is left. The familiarity of address is seen in 'there's nothing going on' and 'God knows how long'. The deadness of the Church in his eyes is seen in his list of the inanimate objects which make up 'another church'. His irreverent attitude is seen in 'some brass and stuff up at the holy end'. Yet his dilemma is also seen at the end—he knows that some gesture is needed, he has no hat to remove, so he takes off his cycle-clips in 'awkward reverence'.

(5) "My lov'd, my honor'd, much respected friend!
No mercenary bard his homage pays;
With honest pride, I scorn each selfish end,
My dearest meed, a friend's esteem and praise:"†

These are the opening lines of a poem in which Robert Burns directly addresses Robert Aiken, his friend and patron, to whom he wished to dedicate the whole poem. Given this situation, how appropriate is the register?

Many modern readers will find it totally inappropriate. They can point to the curiously stilted form of address

*"Church Going" (Philip Larkin)
†"The Cotters Saturday Night" (Robert Burns)

in the first line, more appropriate perhaps to a sermon or a political oration than to a friendly greeting; the elision of the 'e' of the past participle ending; the strange word order—subject, object, verb—of the second line; the use of the archaic word 'meed' for 'reward'; the absence of a verb in the fourth line. It might be maintained that no man could conceivably address a friend, either in speech or in writing, in such an artificial way and yet be sincere in what he says.

Such critics are, of course, right if they expect a poem always to be an exact reproduction of the normal patterns of language. What has to be realised, however, is that Burns was writing according to certain poetic conventions that were completely acceptable in his day. 'Poetic licence' permitted poets to distort the normal rules of grammar, and 'poetic diction' was accepted as being quite different from the diction of other forms of communication. Neither Burns, nor Aiken, nor the readers of the time would have found anything odd in these lines at all. The modern reader might expect here the register of informal address and be disappointed, but the eighteenth century reader would expect, and received, the 'register of poetry'.

This is a serious difficulty for many newcomers to poetry as they read the poetry of earlier centuries. Nowadays there is hardly such a thing as a 'register of poetry'. We expect our poetry to be written in a register appropriate to its situation—a register modified to some extent because it is poetry, but nevertheless recognisable as basically the same as that of any other form of language dealing with a similar situation. Only through experience can the reader learn to accept the poetic conventions of earlier ages.

For examination purposes, however, there need be no problem. All Scottish and most English school examinations can safely be expected to deal with poetry which is, if not contemporary, at least modern—that is, of the twentieth century.

3 Grammar

Poets often draw the reader's attention to something which is particularly significant by departing from the normally-accepted patterns of language. All such departures should be regarded as significant, although sometimes their significance is confined to meeting the requirements of rhyme and rhythm. For example, Wordsworth's 'Simon Lee the Old Huntsman' contains the lines
> "Few months of life has he in store,
> As he to you will tell,"

instead of the more normal 'as he will tell (to) you'. Here we should not be seeking to find out why he wished to lay special emphasis on 'tell'. He was merely seeking a line to rhyme with
> "For still, the more he works, the more
> Do his weak ankles swell."

This is, in fact, an example of verse where departure from the normal is an indication of poverty rather than richness of poetic technique.

Assuming that the poem is of a higher quality than this, we must regard all departures from the normal patterns as significant. But what are the normal patterns? Here it will be necessary to devote a little space to some essential explanations, in order to make it possible to recognise and describe these patterns in a simple and brief way.

GRAMMAR AND LEXIS

A fundamental distinction must be made at once between the two terms grammar and lexis. This distinction can best be shown by an example:—

The *careless boy kicked* a *ball* through our *window*. Every word here represents a choice made by the user of the words. In the positions filled by the words in italics, the choice was made from an infinite number of possibilities—what is called an open set. No one could list all the items that might appear between 'The' and

18

'boy', for example, and the same is true of each of the
other items in italic. When we discuss words of this
kind, we are discussing 'lexis', and considering the 'lexical
choice' that has been made.

The other positions, however, are filled from a strictly
limited list of possibilities. It is possible—though perhaps
with some difficulty—to make a list of every word in the
language which could possibly occur in the positions
occupied by 'The', 'a', 'through', and 'our'. This is
also true of the ending '-ed' after 'kick'. Items which
are filled from a finite stock of possibilities—a closed
system—are the concern of 'grammar', and we say that
a 'grammatical choice' has been made.
Here is another example:—

My *mother* was *going* to the *dairy* for *milk* and *butter*.
Once again, the words in italic are lexical items, and the
other words (and '-ing') are grammatical items.

In this section of the book, we shall be concerned with
everything except the author's lexical choices, which will
be the subject of the next section.

SENTENCE PATTERNS

Having distinguished between grammar and lexis, we
must now consider some of the structural patterns that
are common in English. Only the patterns which are
most important for our purposes will be discussed. The
terminology used is different from some of the terminology
of traditional grammar, and is based on modern linguistic
theory.

(1) The basic pattern of the statement in English is
known as SP (i.e. Subject followed by Predicator):—

    S   P

He / ran.

Sometimes a third item, C (Complement), is necessary
to complete the statement:—

    S   P   C

He / ran / a good race.

A fourth item, A (Adjunct), can also appear as required:—

    S   P   C   A

He / ran / a good race / in the championships.

The item A can occur several times:—

    S   P   C   A   A

He / ran / a good race / in the championships / last week.

The only limit on the number of Adjuncts used is the need to preserve intelligibility and style. Where several occur, one A is sometimes transferred to a different position, usually at the beginning of the sentence:—

    A   S   P   C   A

Last week / he / ran / a good race / in the champion-

        A

ships / at Meadowbank.

The basic pattern, then, is SPCA, with items C and A not always present, and item A capable of appearing several times, not always in the same place.

(2) The examples of sentence pattern given so far have all been sentences which consist of one clause—that is, the items S and P occur once only. Such a sentence is called a *Simple Sentence*. There are, however, sentences in which one of the items S, C, or A is expressed not by a *group*, but by a *clause*, this clause itself consisting of some version of the SPCA structure. For example:—

    A   S   P   C

Last week / he / said / that he had run a good race in the championships.

Here the item C consists of the *binder* 'that' followed by:—

    S   P   C   A

he / had run / a good race / in the championships. Such a sentence is called a *Complex Sentence*. Here is another example:—

         A   S   P   C

When I met him / he / said / that he had run a good race in the championships.

In this case, not only is the item C expounded by an SPCA clause, but the item A is also a clause, consisting of the binder 'when' followed by

    S   P   C

I / met / him.

In some sentences there is an even greater degree of complexity:—

```
        S      P                        C
```
He / said / that he had run a good race when he broke the record.

The item C consists of the binder 'that' followed by
```
        S       P          C             A
```
he / had run / a good race / when he broke the record.

In turn, the item A in this expression also consists of a clause, made up of a binder ('when') followed by
```
        S       P        C
```
he / broke / the record.

(3) One other sentence pattern must be mentioned This is the sentence, complete in itself, which contains no verb—that is, the item P is not present. Such a sentence is very common in speech, especially in reply to a question:—

Where were you last night?—At home.

Did you stay in all night?—Yes.

Obviously 'At home' and 'Yes' are complete utterances, and must be called sentences. The item P is not present, however, so it is not possible to describe them in the usual terms of SPCA. Such a sentence is sometimes called a minor sentence, as distinct from a major sentence, which is grammatically complete. Its presence in speech is readily accepted, but where it occurs in written English we can often attach special significance to it.

THE NOMINAL GROUP

The nominal group is equivalent to the pronoun, noun, and noun phrase of traditional grammar, and includes all those terms. It can best be defined as the item in the SPCA structure which always occurs in the position S, very often—but not always—occurs in the position C, and sometimes occurs in the position A when preceded by a preposition. In the sentence below, the nominal groups are in italic.

My young cousin said that *he* had run *a good race* in *the championships.*

When the nominal group consists of a single word, that word is known as the *Headword* (H). This word carries out the 'naming' function of the group. In addition

21

to the *Headword*, certain words may appear before it, and they are called *Modifiers* (M). Thus the group 'the old men' can be written as

    M   H

The old / men.

When the group includes something appearing after the Headword, this is known as a Qualifier (Q). Thus:—

    M   H   Q

The old / men / in the park.

The structure of the nominal group can thus be defined as

(M) H (Q)

    Once the whole nominal group has been used, it can, of course, be replaced in succeeding sentences by a single pronoun. Thus we can say:—

    The old men in the park were happy. *They* were enjoying the sunshine. *It* warmed their hearts.

In normal usage, in order that the words 'they' and 'it' should convey any meaning, we must have the earlier reference to 'the old men in the park' and 'the sunshine'.

    The structure of the nominal group can be very important in English for different purposes. For example we often find in semi-official, 'governmental' language, and in newspaper headlines, a pronounced use of noun-adjectives as modifiers in a nominal group:—

    The *Scottish Certificate of Education Examination Board* Offices.

    Home Rule Talks Deadlock

The items in italic one would normally expect to see as nouns, yet here they are used as part of the item M.

    All forms of persuasive language, especially advertising, tend to use very heavy nominal groups:—

           M   H

Their exclusive long-life weather-proof / soles / made

    Q

of pure leather / are guaranteed to give satisfaction.

    So far in this section, all that has been done has been to establish some idea of what are the normal patterns of English. As has already been said, poetry often makes use of a departure from the normal patterns with striking effect. It is now time to consider some such departures from the normal, and to see how they can add to our understanding of the poem.

MEANING SUGGESTED BY GRAMMATICAL CHOICE

It might be thought that meaning is carried almost exclusively by a writer's lexical choice, but in poetry especially the grammatical choice is often very interesting and revealing. A good example of this can be found in Philip Larkin's poem 'Church Going'. In this poem, Larkin describes the passing of the Church as a vital influence on men's lives. He speculates on the future, when only ruins will mark where churches once stood, in the words,

"Grass, weedy pavement, brambles, buttress, sky,
A shape less recognizable each week,
A purpose more obscure."

Here the poet departs from the normal convention by not using the word 'and' to link together all these items in a list. Yet further on in the same poem, recognising the importance that the Church once had for all men, he refers to

".............—marriage, and birth,
And death, and thoughts of these—"

Here he departs from the normal in the opposite direction, by using 'and' more often than convention allows. Presumably he has a reason. To him, 'grass, weedy pavement, brambles, buttress, sky' represents a state of affairs very different from 'marriage, and birth, and death, and thoughts of these'. The first, objective, function of Practical Criticism is to be aware of this difference. The second, subjective, function is to decide what significance to attach to the difference, and here each critic must make up his own mind. In this case it could be held, for example, that the absence of connectives in the first list is an indication of a state of disintegration, which is contrasted with the almost excessive continuity suggested by the frequent use of 'and' in the second list. At any rate, it is clear that here is a case where 'grammar' contributes something important to meaning.

A similar instance can be seen in Ted Hughes's poem
'Thrushes', in which the poet brings out effectively the
sheer efficiency in killing of what is often thought of as a
rather nice, gentle creature. At one point Hughes
describes how the thrushes

"............... —with a start, a bounce, a stab
Overtake the instant and drag out some writhing
thing."

Had he inserted the word 'and' between 'bounce' and
'stab', as most prose writers would have done, what
would have been lost to the reader?

A different but equally significant breach of grammatical convention can be seen in another poem by Philip
Larkin, 'Mr Bleaney', in which the poet—either as
himself or under the shelter of a persona—rents the rather
seedy lodgings of the recently deceased Mr Bleaney. The
drabness of the room is brought out in the lines

"Bed, upright chair, sixty-watt bulb, no hook
Behind the door, no room for books or bags—
'I'll take it'."

What is striking here is the absence of the article 'a'
before 'bed', 'chair', and 'bulb'. Probably two effects
can be detected—first, the quick fleeting inventory that
the speaker makes before deciding to take the room, and
secondly the cold depressing bleakness of such a room.

The presence or absence of the article can have a
much more pronounced effect on meaning. A well
known example is to be found in the following passage
from 'Journey of the Magi', by T. S. Eliot:—

"   were we led all that way for
Birth or Death? There was a birth, certainly,
We had evidence and no doubt. I had seen birth
and death,
But had thought they were different, this Birth was
Hard and bitter agony for us, like Death, our death."

It is very instructive here to consider every occurrence
of the words 'birth' and 'death', and to decide how the
meaning is affected in each case by the presence or
absence of the article (and also the capital letters).

This departure from grammatical convention must not
be thought of as something modern. Three hundred

years ago, James Shirley, in 'Death the Leveller', pointed out that men of all ranks and classes must come at last to the same end, in the familiar lines,

"   Sceptre and Crown
          Must tumble down,
      And in the dust be equal made
      With the poor crooked scythe and spade."

'Sceptre and Crown' clearly represent human grandeur, and 'scythe and spade' represent the more humble walks of life. It is interesting to notice that the lofty, remote state of royalty is contrasted with the ordinariness of the common peasant not only by means of the capital letters, but also by means of the omission of 'the'.

One final example must suffice here. In 'Death in Leamington', John Betjeman describes the rather lonely and pathetic death of a respectable, even prosperous lady of the middle classes. At one point there occurs the line

"And Nurse came in with the tea-things".

What would be the effect had Betjeman written

"And the nurse came in with the tea-things"?

MEANING SUGGESTED BY CLAUSE STRUCTURE

We have already seen that the normal SPCA pattern of the clause permits variation of the position of A as an aid to good style. In poetry, however, we find a great deal of variation for other reasons. Sometimes the patterns are varied on grounds of convenience, merely to fit the rhyme and rhythm of the poem, and with no implications as to meaning. Much more important from our point of view is the way in which a poet can give special emphasis to a word or phrase by the deliberate adoption of an unusual pattern.

In 'Church Going', for example, Larkin uses the line

"A serious house on serious earth it is".

This is, in fact, a CASP structure. The placing of C, 'a serious house', at the beginning of the sentence gives it great emphasis, and this emphasis is of course reinforced by the second use of the word 'serious' immediately afterwards.

Earlier in the same poem we have the lines
"   Back at the door
I sign the book, donate an Irish sixpence,
Reflect the place was not worth stopping for.

Yet stop I did:"

Several points of techniques combine to draw our attention to the important statement—that however much the poet is convinced of the uselessness of the Church, there remains something that draws him to it. First we have a series of actions whose aimlessness is brought out by the absence of the connective 'and'. Then the important phrase is introduced in a position of great emphasis—the first words of a new stanza. It is made to stand out more by the strong pause after it, indicated by the colon. Further attention is drawn to it by the fact that 'stop' is a repetition of the last stressed syllable of the preceding stanza. Then the poet has chosen to use the emphatic form of the past tense—'did stop' rather than 'stopped'. Finally, to complete the effect, he has departed from the normal clause pattern by placing the item S ('I') between the two elements of the item P and reversing the normal order of these two elements. Compare the effects produced by each of the following:—

Yet I stopped.

Yet I did stop.

Yet stop I did.

Ted Hughes's poem 'Thrushes', as we have seen, is one in which the poet seeks to bring out an aspect of these birds which would never occur to the sentimental—their ruthless, machine-like efficiency as killers. In the very opening of the poem we are shocked into this realisation:—
"Terrifying are the attent sleek thrushes on the
lawn,".

By adopting the unusual pattern CPS—the very opposite of the normal pattern—the poet concentrates our attention on the word that matters most—'terrifying'.

The same poet, in 'An Otter', demonstrates the effectiveness of an even more radical departure from the normal patterns. One stanza is typical of the whole poem:—

> "Brings the legend of himself
> From before wars or burials, in spite of hounds and
>   vermin-poles;
> Does not take root like the badger. Wanders, cries;
> Gallops along land he no longer belongs to;
> Re-enters the water by melting.

The striking feature here is that in all the main clauses the subject has been omitted altogether, yet conventional language demands that in major clauses, whatever else may be present, the items S and P are essential. Something of the mysteriousness of the otter is brought out by this device—a creature of the land which is more at home in the water, a creature which seems to endure for ever, yet one which has no fixed home of its own.

These examples all bring out the important fact that, while a poet's meaning is conveyed by the words he uses, the full implications of what he is saying are often brought out by the order in which he uses them. Unfortunately, poets have often departed from the normal clause patterns without producing this additional effect. Early conventions in poetry permitted variations which served to give regularity to rhyme and rhythm, but which added little or nothing to meaning. Gray's 'Elegy Written in a Country Churchyard' is full of examples:—

> "And all the air a solemn stillness holds"
> "Their furrow oft the stubborn glebe has broke"
> "Hands that the rod of empire might have swayed".

In these cases little or nothing is added to meaning. Indeed, in the last case, there could be some doubt as to the meaning—do the hands sway the rod, or does the rod sway the hands? We can easily work out which meaning is intended, but the clause pattern itself does nothing to help.

Such a convention is no longer acceptable in poetry. When a modern poet departs from the normal clause patterns, we can safely assume that there is some significance in his departure. In approaching the works of older writers, however, we must accept the fact that they were writing under different conventions, and we must not look to them for precisely the same effects as are given by modern poetry.

So far we have considered structure within the clause. Now we must consider the structure of the whole sentence. Once again, we must look for any means by which sentence structure can be seen to make some contribution to the total meaning of the poem.

In 'Hawk Roosting', Ted Hughes conveys the arrogance of the hawk, secure in its physical superiority over all others, and confident that the world exists for its particular benefit. This arrogant confidence can be clearly seen in the last stanza:—

> "The sun is behind me.
> Nothing has changed since I began.
> My eye has permitted no change.
> I am going to keep things like this."

Apart from the second sentence, which contains two clauses, we have a series of short, blunt, simple sentences, each stopping with the end of the line. The hard, ruthless effect is at once noticeable.

It is interesting to compare the sentence structure of the opening lines of 'Church Going' with that of the closing stanza:—

(a) "Once I am sure there's nothing going on
> I step inside, letting the door thud shut.
> Another church: matting, seats, and stone,
> And little books; sprawlings of flowers, cut
> For Sunday, brownish now; some brass and stuff
> Up at the holy end; the small neat organ;
> And a tense, musty, unignorable silence,
> Brewed God knows how long. Hatless, I take off
> My cycle-clips in awkward reverence,
> Move forward, run my hand around the font."

(b) "A serious house on serious earth it is,
> In whose blent air all our compulsions meet,
> Are recognized, and robed as destinies.
> And that much never can be obsolete,
> Since someone will forever be surprising
> A hunger in himself to be more serious,
> And gravitating with it to this ground,
> Which, he once heard, was proper to grow wise in
> If only that so many dead lie round."

In the first passage, we have three sentences. The first occupies two lines, and is complex. The second occupies the next six lines, and is a simple sentence, though lacking a main verb. Finally there is a sentence consisting of three main clauses, strung together without the use of 'and'. Thus, apart from the first two lines, we have no complexity of sentence structure.

In the second passage, things are very different. The first sentence consists of a main clause with a combination of three clauses dependent on it. The remaining six lines consist of a single very complex sentence, consisting of a main clause and no fewer than five dependent clauses.

The simple structure of the first passage is indicative of what the poet is describing at that point—a series of almost aimless actions and apparently useless objects. On the other hand, his comments in the final stanza are of a much more complex nature, and some of their complexity is reflected in the complex sentence structure he uses.

Something quite different can be seen in the following passage from Tennyson's 'Morte d'Arthur':—

"Then quickly rose Sir Bedivere, and ran,
And, leaping down the ridges lightly, plunged
Among the bulrush beds, and clutched the sword,
And strongly wheeled and threw it."

Here we have no fewer than six main clauses, with the connective 'and' used five times to join the six together. This frequency of the use of 'and' is very unusual, but we have only to read the lines aloud to realise how effective it is in suggesting a man desperate to carry out a distasteful task as quickly as possible, allowing himself no time for thought and a possible change of mind.

In part of Thomas Blackburn's 'Hospital for Defectives', we can see again a series of 'and' clauses used rather more frequently than might be expected:—

"For all things seem to figure out
The stirrings of your heart,
And two men pick the turnips up
And two men pull the cart;
And yet between the four of them

E

No word is ever said
Because the yeast was not put in
Which makes the human bread.
But three men stare on vacancy
And one man strokes his knees;
What is the meaning to be found
In such dark vowels as these?"

As we read some of these lines we are conscious of a series
of actions performed without thought and without
feeling by men deprived from birth of the powers of
thought and feeling, and part of this consciousness comes
to us by means of the sentence structure employed.

Some mention has already been made of sentences
without verbs. Such sentences can be a very effective
way of communicating meaning. John Masefield's very
well known poem 'Cargoes' is a good example. It consists of three stanzas, each of parallel construction. The
first stanza will suffice as illustration:—

"Quinquireme of Nineveh from distant Ophir,
Rowing home to haven in sunny Palestine,
With a cargo of ivory,
And apes and peacocks,
Sandalwood, cedarwood, and sweet white wine."

Here, what appears to be a statement is in reality no
more than a nominal group, with the Headword 'Quinquireme' and all the rest Qualifiers. The second and
third stanzas are similar nominal groups relating to
'Stately Spanish galleon' and 'Dirty British coaster'.

The first stage in Practical Criticism is, of course, the
objective recording of phenomena such as this. After
that, each reader must decide for himself what the
phenomenon conveys to him. Here it could be thought
that the poet is giving three separate 'pictures' on a
related theme, such as 'Shipping through the Ages'. It
is much more likely, however, that the three stanzas
combine to make one statement in an indirect way—
perhaps one about the comparative values of the three
cargoes, perhaps one about the timelessness of man's
basic activities despite the superficial differences brought
about by time and fashion.

One verbless sentence in 'Church Going' has already been quoted:—

> "Another church: matting, seats, and stone,
> And little books; sprawlings of flowers, cut
> For Sunday, brownish now; some brass and stuff
> Up at the holy end; the small neat organ;
> And a tense, musty, unignorable silence,
> Brewed God knows how long."

Perhaps no complete grammatical statement is made here because no statement is intended. What we have is a thought process set down on paper. The thought is expressed by 'Another church:'. After the colon, we have the random observations as the poet stands inside the door and lets his eye range round the interior of the building.

Ted Hughes also uses the verbless sentence in 'Thrushes':—

> "No indolent procrastinations and no yawning stares,
> No sighs or head-scratchings. Nothing but bounce
>   and stab
> And a ravening second."

Here again, what is being made is not a statement but a detached observation, and the sentence structure chosen expresses this perfectly.

Any unusual sentence structure should strike the reader, and its significance should be sought. One final example will be given in the last two stanzas of Philip Larkin's 'Mr Bleaney'. After describing the drab room occupied by the late Mr Bleaney, and speculating on the equally drab shape taken by his life, the poet ends with:—

> "But if he stood and watched the frigid wind
> Tousling the clouds, lay on the fusty bed
> Telling himself that this was home, and grinned,
> And shivered, without shaking off the dread
>
> That how we live measures our own nature,
> And at his age having no more to show
> Than one hired box should make him pretty sure
> He warranted no better, I don't know."

After such a complex array of subordinate clauses, we come at last to the main clause, only to experience some-

thing of an anti-climax—the colloquial 'I don't know'—
as if the very thought of such a bleak existence defies any
firm statement on the part of the poet.

MEANING SUGGESTED BY NOMINAL GROUPS

The structure of nominal groups in poetry is often a
matter of great interest. We often find some kind of
disturbance of the expected order of words, for example.
Thus in Wilfred Gibson's poem 'The Plough' there occurs
the phrase 'the rascal thieves and black' to describe the
birds which attack the farmer's crop and have to be
scared away. The position of 'black' is curious, and
certainly serves to draw our attention to the phrase, but
in this case we may feel that there is nothing much for
our attention to be drawn to. Sometimes, however, such
a disturbance of word order can be much more effective.
'Esther's Tomcat', by Ted Hughes, contains the lines

"   he yawns wide red,
Fangs fine as a lady's needle and bright."

An almost surgical sharpness is what the poet wants to
convey, and the extra emphasis given to 'bright' by its
unexpected position aids his purpose, whereas in Gibson's
poem there was no particular point in emphasising the
predators' blackness—it was their thieving that mattered,
not their colour. Another good example of effective
writing occurs in T. S. Eliot's 'Journey of the Magi'.
The early part of the poem deals with the tedious,
wearisome nature of the journey, and all the unpleasant-
ness that had to be faced. One phrase occurs—'the cities
hostile and the towns unfriendly'—which places adjectives after their nouns, putting emphasis on the adjectives
rather than on the nouns, and thus contributing to the
unpleasant effect Eliot desired.

Sometimes we may find a heavy concentration of
Modifiers before the Headword, and we may be able to
assign some significance to this. The American poet,
Robert Lowell, in 'Waking in the Blue', describes his
experiences in a mental hospital, where, like the other
inmates, he seemed to find some compensation for mental

disorder in taking pride in physical health. There occurs the line

"I strut in my turtle-necked French sailor's jersey"
which brings out well this self-conscious awareness of fine physical appearance.

Another good example occurs in 'On the Move', by Thom Gunn, which deals with the young, rootless, black-jacketed motor-cyclists of modern times. Here we have two lines,

"On motorcycles, up the road, they come:
Small, black, as flies hanging in heat, the Boys".
The second line is a nominal group expanding the pronoun 'they' in the first line. The structure of the group, with the Headword 'Boys' coming at the end of a long series of Modifiers, brings out effectively the distant appearance, the closer approach, and the arrival of these modern wanderers.

Some other examples of extensive modification of the Headword follow, the reader being invited to decide for himself what effect is produced.

(a) Philip Larkin, in 'The Whitsun Weddings', describing the early stages of a journey by train:—

"The river's level drifting breadth began."

(b) Ted Hughes, in 'Thrushes', describing these apparently gentle but actually fierce creatures:—
"   a poised
Dark deadly eye,".

(c) Wilfred Owen, in 'Anthem for Doomed Youth', describing the slaughter of the First World War:—

"Only the stuttering rifle's rapid rattle".

Another interesting feature in Modifiers is the surprising use of a noun as Modifier. Nouns are often used for this purpose in English—stone walls and glass bottles are everyday examples—but in poetry we often find something strikingly unusual. Thus Ted Hughes talks about the thrushes' '*bullet* and automatic purpose' as they strike their targets, the worms. The same poet, in 'Pike', describes the cannibal tendencies of these fish by telling how three were kept together in a tank, the three suddenly became two, and finally one,

"With a *sag* belly and the grin it was born with."

In such cases, the poet's purpose is one of surprise. By using a word in this unusual way, he draws our attention to it, and the meaning of the expression becomes clearer simply by its being noticed.

The use of Qualifiers after the Headword can also be very illuminating. In 'The Whitsun Weddings', Philip Larkin seems at times to be ridiculing the social awkwardness of the working classes on formal occasions such as weddings. Among the places where the wedding receptions are held he mentions 'banquet-halls up yards'. Here the incongruity of the Modifier 'banquet-' and the Qualifier 'up yards' appearing together helps to bring out the incongruity of people dressed in a style to which they are not accustomed taking part in a social ceremony which is an imitation of the social ceremonies of their 'betters'.

A very different use of Qualifiers is found in Yeats's 'The Second Coming', in which the poet has a vision of some powerful, inexorable force which is setting out to restore order to a world in a state verging on chaos. He describes this as

"A shape with lion body and the head of a man,
A gaze blank and pitiless as the sun".

Somehow the lengthy Qualifiers of the very impersonal words 'shape' and 'gaze' seem to bring out this very impersonality and inexorability. Incidentally, within the Qualifier of the first nominal group there occur two separate nominal groups—'lion body' and 'the head of a man'. It would be interesting to speculate why these two groups should be so different. Why not

"with the body of a lion and the head of a man"

or

"with lion body and man head"?

The poet's choice was obviously deliberate. What significance may lie behind his choice of words?

Perhaps the most interesting of all the peculiarities of the nominal group in poetry is the case of the pronoun which refers to nothing that has gone before. It has already been shown that, once a nominal group has been stated, it can afterwards be replaced by a pronoun.

(*The old men in the park* were happy. *They* were enjoying the sunshine.) In poetry, however, especially in modern poetry, we often find the curious case of the pronoun occurring without any previous reference at all. Obviously when we notice this our interest must be stimulated, and we must try to decide what effect this device has for us. A few examples will be given, with suggested interpretations, but many more can be found by even a casual glance through the works of most modern poets, and in each case the reader must decide for himself what to make of the device—is it merely a trick of style, or is it truly significant?

    (a) "On motorcycles, up the road, *they* come:
        Small, black, as flies hanging in heat, the Boys"
                    (Thom Gunn, 'On the Move')

'They' are at first remote and anonymous. Then they come nearer, and at last emerge as 'the Boys', capital letter and all.

    (b) "The eye can hardly pick *them* out"
                    (Philip Larkin, 'At Grass')

Here again, there is the idea of the anonymity of former racehorses now in a state of retirement. Indeed, the first stanza ends with 'anonymous again', and the rest of the poem goes on to contrast the former glory attached to their names with the fact that they have now 'slipped their names'.

    (c) "   Once we started, though,
        We passed *them*, grinning and pomaded, girls
        In parodies of fashion, heels and veils,"
              (Philip Larkin, 'The Whitsun Weddings')

The anonymity of 'them' suggests the sheer multiplicity of the wedding parties, each one indistinguishable from the others.

    (d) "*She* dwelt among the untrodden ways
        Beside the springs of Dove;
      A maid whom there were none to praise,
        And very few to love."
          (William Wordsworth, 'The Lost Love')

This example is introduced to show that, while the device is particularly common in modern poetry, it is not new. In this case, the anonymity of 'she' suggests the obscurity of the life she led. At the end of the poem she is given a name—Lucy—and this brings home to us her reality, and increases the sadness at the thought that she was loved, is now dead, and is bitterly mourned.

MEANING SUGGESTED BY OTHER NON-LEXICAL FEATURES

This final section will be concerned with various devices for conveying and emphasising meaning in poetry which do not fit into the categories already discussed.

(1) *Unusual compounds*

These have always been a feature of poetry, though perhaps they have become more common since the late nineteenth century, when Gerard Manley Hopkins used them to great advantage. Unusual compounds serve a double purpose—first, they attract attention by their very strangeness, and secondly by their use of compressed grammatical structure they are heavily loaded with meaning expressed in the most economical way. Thus, when Hopkins, in 'The Windhover', talks of the 'dapple-dawn-drawn Falcon' we at once notice the expression, and then we realise how many words would be required to say the same thing in a more normal fashion. The same poet, in 'Inversnaid', describing the foam-covered course of a brown mountain burn, uses the words

"A windpuff-bonnet of fawn-froth".

Later in the same poem he refers to the 'beadbonny ash' that stands by the side of the burn.

Countless examples of unusual compounds could be quoted from modern poetry, but a few will suffice, all picked at random from the poems of Philip Larkin:—

"Beside grain-scattered streets, barge-crowded waters"

"Vast Sunday-full and organ-frowned-on spaces"

"hold-it smiles"

"short-shadowed cattle"

"my three-quarters-empty train"

(2) *Unusual grammatical categories*

Just as the unusual compound draws attention to itself by its unexpectedness, so does the use of a word with a function quite different from its normal. Thus when Kingsley Amis, in 'Something Nasty in the Bookshop', asks

>"Should poets bicycle-pump the human heart
>Or squash it flat?"

we are struck at once by his use of what is usually a noun as a particularly ugly-sounding verb.

Attention has already been drawn to the adjectival use of nouns as Modifiers in nominal groups, as in the case of Ted Hughes's 'bullet and automatic purpose'. All sorts of other surprising uses can readily be found. Here are a few examples:—

>"In gleaming jackets *trophied* with the dust"
>
>>(Thom Gunn, 'On the Move')
>
>"With webbed feet and long *ruddering* tail"
>
>>(Ted Hughes, 'An Otter')
>
>"Three we kept behind glass,
>*Jungled* in weed."
>
>>(Ted Hughes, 'Pike')
>
>"Canals with *floatings* of industrial froth"
>
>>(Philip Larkin, 'The Whitsun Weddings')
>
>"*sprawlings* of flowers"
>
>>(Philip Larkin, 'Church Going')

(3) *Punctuation and other markings*

Sometimes in poetry punctuation requires careful examination. Compare, for example, these two short extracts from 'Thrushes':—

(a) 　　　　　　a poised
　　　Dark deadly eye,"

(b) 　"　　　　　—with a start, a bounce, a stab"

In the first case commas have been omitted where they might have been expected. In the second case they have been used, even after 'bounce', where one might have expected the comma to be replaced by 'and'. This difference is obviously intended, and it is for the reader to decide what effect is produced in each case, and how the effect would be altered by different punctuation.

Any mark—or its absence—can be significant. Not for nothing, surely, did Philip Larkin call his poem 'Church Going' rather than 'Church-going'. With the hyphen,

F

the title would suggest going to church in order to participate in its ceremonies, whereas Larkin describes entering a church—"Once I am sure there's nothing going on"—as a detached observer. Indeed, when we have read the poem we may come to the conclusion that the word 'Going' has been used to describe the Church itself rather than the visitor.

Capital letters in unexpected places can also convey something of the poet's meaning. John Betjeman has a poem, 'The Planster's Vision', in which he attacks the way in which modern planning sometimes seems to be opposed to man's essential individuality. Part of the poem goes as follows:—

"Remove those cottages, a huddled throng!
  Too many babies have been born in there,
  Too many coffins, bumping down the stair,
Carried the old their garden paths along.

  I have a Vision of the Future, chum,
  The workers' flats in fields of soya beans"

The use of capitals gives the effect of some idealistic theory, or something extracted from a political manifesto, but certainly nothing to do with the warm bloodstream of ordinary people's lives.

It would be pointless to attempt to categorise, with examples, all the ways in which the presence or absence of punctuation and other marks can give illumination to a piece of poetry. It may, however, be enough to have drawn attention to the need for the closest scrutiny of even such apparently trivial details.

(4) *Line divisions*

This section will be brief, not because there is little to be said about it, but because there is almost too much to be said about it for the limits of this book.

The point at which the poet stops one line and goes on to the next is, of course, dictated by the form he has adopted for his poem. Very often he so arranges things that the line division coincides with a grammatical division, and this is often indicated by punctuation. It can be interesting, however, to notice when the sense of a line runs straight on to the next line, and what effect is produced as a result. More will be said on this subject in the part of the book dealing with Sound Patterns. In the meantime, it may be sufficient to give an illustration from a poem about which much has already been said— 'Church Going'.

In the first stanza, almost all of the lines run together, almost as the random observations run together in the poet's mind. Even the end of the stanza does not mark a stopping-point:—

> Hatless, I take off
> My cycle-clips in awkward reverence,
>
> Move forward, run my hand around the font."

Throughout the second stanza, the same pattern continues—stops occurring apparently at random, quite unconnected with the line divisions. Then this stanza ends with a full stop, and this indicates the end of the first part of the poem, the narrative part. Something new begins with 'Yet stop I did' in the third stanza, and the run-on lines of the opening stanzas have contributed some part to the means by which this important phrase is made to stand out clearly.

(5) *A repeated phrase*

The last topic to be discussed in this chapter is really not a matter exclusively of grammar or of lexis or of sound patterns, but contains elements of all three. It concerns a key phrase, repeated at different points in the poem, usually with some very slight alteration at the end which somehow completes the statement.

Yeats often made use of a refrain at the end of each stanza, rather in the manner of the folk-song, but carrying more meaning than the repeated folk-song refrain, which is often no more than a jingle for the audience to join in. In 'A Song', for example, he laments the onset of old age in three short stanzas, followed by a refrain,

> "O who could have foretold
> That the heart grows old?"

At the end of the last stanza, however, this refrain is very slightly altered, to

> "For who could have foretold
> That the heart grows old?"

Once again, each reader must decide for himself how much more final this alteration makes the refrain.

Something similar occurs in 'The Welsh Hill Country', by R. S. Thomas. This time each of the first two stanzas begins with

"Too far for you to see"

and goes on to contrast the usual romantic picture of beautiful countryside with the harsh reality of poverty and disease, both animal and human. The third stanza is subtly altered, beginning

"Too far, too far to see".

Again, each reader must decide for himself how this alteration completes the picture of despair.

A very recent Scottish poem, 'The Coming of the Wee Malkies', by Stephen Mulrine, uses the same device in an apparently jocular fashion. Each of its three stanzas opens by asking

"Whit'll ye dae when the wee Malkies come?"

and then goes on, in the broadest Glasgow dialect, to list every imaginable catastrophe that might threaten the house-proud, well-doing woman, fighting a desperate battle to preserve some standards of decency in the tenement jungle of the Glasgow slums. The first two stanzas end with

"Missis, whit'll ye dae?"

But the last stanza seems to pose the question from some deeper region of the heart—

"Haw missis, whit'll ye dae?"

4   Choice of Words

The previous chapter began by making a fundamental distinction between grammar and lexis. Grammar deals with 'closed systems', lexis with 'open sets'—that is, positions in the sentence where the writer makes his choice from an infinite set of possibilities. In the chapter which follows, we shall be concerned exclusively with lexis—the words the poet actually chooses from this infinite list of possibilities.

LEXICAL CHOICE

Straight away we must discard any idea that there are 'good' words and 'bad' words, words which are poetic and words which are not. The criteria by which a poet's lexical choice is to be judged are

(a) effectiveness, and

(b) appropriateness.

The effectiveness of a word is to be judged by how precisely it conveys the poet's meaning. We are all familiar with the idea that a word such as 'nice' has lost much of its effectiveness through over-use—a nice day, a nice book, a nice person, a nice meal, a nice party. How can any one adjective effectively describe so many different nouns? The skilful writer, and the skilful poet in particular, knows to choose words which are much more effective in conveying his precise meaning. Thus Philip Larkin, in 'Church Going', lets the door 'thud' shut, not 'slam'; the echoes 'snigger' briefly, not 'chuckle'; a few cathedrals are kept 'chronically' on show, not 'permanently'.

In considering the effectiveness of lexical choice, of course, we should waste no time over words to which no particular significance is attached. When Larkin lets the door thud shut, we should not worry about why he chose 'door' instead of 'portal'; when he says 'yet stop I did' we should not ask why he did not use 'halt'; when he talks of women and their 'children' we should not debate the advantage of 'children' over 'offspring'. These words have been chosen simply for their literal meaning, with no other implications. It is only when a word is striking in its effectiveness that it demands our attention.

The appropriateness of a writer's lexical choice is to be judged in relation to the situation and the register adopted. Larkin in church notices 'some brass and stuff up at the holy end'. The terms 'stuff' and 'the holy end' may seem colloquial and irreverent—but they are intended to be so. His choice is entirely appropriate for one who has in fact lost reverence for what the Church once stood for. In sharp contrast, when John Milton, in 'Il Penseroso', seeks to convey the solemnity and grandeur of the Church he rightly rejects any frivolous terms, and adopts a diction appropriate to the register of the situation he has chosen:—

> "But let my due feet never fail
> To walk the studious cloisters pale,
> And love the high-embowéd roof,
> With antique pillars massy proof,
> And storied windows richly dight
> Casting a dim religious light."

Again, of course, in considering the appropriateness of the words chosen we must consider only those words which are particularly striking, and can safely ignore those words—feet, roof, windows, etc.—which in this passage simply mean what they say.

It is only in comparatively recent times that appropriateness to the situation has been given such importance. There was a time when poetry was held to be such a dignified pursuit that it deserved a special diction of its own, quite distinct from that of ordinary prosaic communication. Such diction we label 'poetic diction'. Thus Thomas Gray, writing in the eighteenth century, in 'Ode on the Distant Prospect of Eton College', could describe the action of swimming as

> "   to cleave
> With pliant arm thy glassy wave."

To play with a hoop was

> "To chase the rolling circle's speed",

and to play football was to "urge the flying ball".

At the end of the eighteenth century Wordsworth rebelled against this poetic convention, declaring that the true language of poetry is "a selection of the real language of men in a state of vivid sensation", and that "there neither is nor can be any essential difference between the language of prose and metrical composition." Most modern poets have gone far beyond Wordsworth in their use of the language of ordinary men. To Wordsworth there seemed nothing inappropriate in beginning the monologue of a mother whose son has gone away from home and has lost touch with her in the words,

"Where art thou, my beloved Son,
Where art thou, worse to me than dead!"

Here the diction is not as artificial as that of Gray already quoted, but it is a far cry from Philip Larkin in 'Mr Bleaney', writing in the ordinary colloquial language of our time, with

"   and stub my fags
On the same saucer-souvenir," and
"He kept on plugging at the four aways".

By the very choice of 'stub', 'fags', 'plugging', and 'four aways', Larkin is able to suggest something of the drabness and ordinariness of the life led by such as Mr Bleaney, and to suggest how incomplete such a life is.

The use of colloquial vocabulary is one of the main marks of modern poetry. The introduction of colloquial language has been a gradual process—Browning in his dramatic monologues, the poets of the First World War, Yeats in his later poems—but perhaps T. S. Eliot can be singled out as something of an innovator in this direction. One of his most serious poems, 'The Waste Land', includes lines such as

"Now Albert's coming back, make yourself a bit smart.
He'll want to know what you done with that money
                                he gave you
To get yourself some teeth. He did, I was there.
You have them all out, Lil, and get a nice set,
He said, I swear, I can't bear to look at you.
And no more can't I, I said, and think of poor Albert,
He's been in the army four years, he wants a good
                                time,

And if you don't give it him, there's others will, I
said."

After Eliot, modern poets have been entirely liberated
from the notion that important poetry requires a diction
that is dignified. Louis MacNeice, for example, in
'Bagpipe Music', sums up the preoccupation of the
Thirties with empty materialism in the line
"All we want is a bank balance and a bit of skirt in a
taxi."

Modern poetry takes colloquialism for granted, provided
that colloquialism is appropriate to the situation. The
use of colloquial language, when it is observed, should
always be related to the situation, and it should be
accepted or rejected on grounds of appropriateness and
nothing else—what does it contribute to the meaning of
the poem, not is it poetic language?

Just as in grammar we are particularly interested when
the poet departs from the normal patterns, so in lexis
we are particularly interested when the poet departs
strikingly from the register he has chosen. We are very
concerned with the fact that a poem is written in colloquial language, but we are even more concerned when in
such a poem a particular word is used which represents
a sudden departure from the colloquial. In the same way,
we may notice that a poem is written in very formal
language, and the sudden use of one colloquial term may
force our attention on that word. John Betjeman's poem
'The Planster's Vision' has already been referred to. The
language of the first stanza is in a sense neutral, neither
particularly 'literary' nor particularly colloquial, merely
language. Then the second stanza opens with

"I have a Vision of the Future, chum."
At once the incongruity of the very colloquial 'chum' is
noticed. It seems to suggest that in the planner's eyes
we are all the same, drab and uniform, with no place left
for individuality. Not only that, but the uniformity
imposed on us will be a cultural levelling-down rather
than a levelling-up towards articulateness.

A good example occurs also in Philip Larkin's poem
'Broadcast'. Here the narrator is attending an orchestral

concert not because he is keen on the music but because he is keen on the girl he is with, a girl who is obviously an enthusiast for culture. His failure to appreciate the beauty of sound which he hears, and indeed his suspicion that many of the audience are there merely because it is 'the right thing to do', is well brought in

"Cascades of monumental slithering'

as he describes the sound of the massed strings of the orchestra. Much of the effect is produced by the incongruity of a word like 'slithering' appearing in close association with more 'poetic' words like 'cascades' and 'monumental'.

The highly colloquial passage already quoted from 'The Waste Land' ("Now Albert's coming back,") is striking in itself, but it is even more striking when we compare it with the opening lines of the same section of the poem:—

"The Chair she sat in, like a burnished throne,
Glowed on the marble, where the glass
Held up by standards wrought with fruited vines
From which a golden Cupidon peeped out
(Another hid his eyes behind his wing)
Doubled the flames of sevenbranched candelabra
Reflecting light upon the table as
The glitter of her jewels rose to meet it,
From satin cases poured in rich profusion;"

The change of register is at once apparent. When we read the whole poem, however, we realise that the rather gracious language of the opening passage conceals below its surface a way of life that is no less empty, and indeed squalid, than the obviously squalid life conveyed by the final passage. The startling change of register serves to draw our attention to these two passages, and so enables us to make this discovery about them.

Apart from colloquialisms, any word which causes us some surprise in its context deserves our attention. Presumably the poet intends us first to be surprised by the word, and then to consider its implications. This is, in fact, a way of giving emphasis to a word of some importance. Words of various kinds may be used for this purpose—rare words, archaic words, dialect words, for

G

example. All cases noticed should be regarded with interest. Philip Larkin, in 'Toads', describes the daily necessity of working for a living as a toad which squats on our lives. One line occurs:—

"Its hunkers are heavy as hard luck."

The dialect term 'hunkers' immediately stands out, and we quickly realise how effective it is in conveying the sheer weight and the ugly nature of the brute that restricts our freedom.

Ted Hughes, in 'Wind', talks of "the *brunt* wind that dented the balls of my eyes". In 'Thrushes' he writes "Though he bends to be *blent* in the prayer". In 'Esther's Tomcat' he says that the cat "*grallochs* odd dogs on the quiet". R. S. Thomas, in 'A Peasant', describes this crude, earthy figure, who leans forward "to *gob* in the fire". Burns's Tam o' Shanter is a "blethering, blustering, drunken *blellum*". In each case, the reader is forced at least to notice the word. What it suggests to him he must then decide for himself.

DENOTATION AND CONNOTATION

In this section we shall be concerned with the meaning of words. The term 'meaning' may seem simple, but in fact the concept of meaning is very complex. For our purposes, however, we can simplify matters by stating that a word often carries both a denotation and a connotation. *Denotation* is concerned with the simple meaning of a word in its context—'he walked across the street' is quite different in denotation from 'he looked across the street', whereas it denotes something similar to 'he strolled across the street' but 'strolled' and 'walked' are different in connotation. *Connotation* is concerned not simply with the literal meaning of a word, but with all that is implied in addition to its primary meaning—all that we associate with a word, whether in approval or disapproval.

He *stepped* to the window.

He *strode* to the window.

He *stolled* to the window.

He *strutted* to the window.

All the words in italic *denote* 'walked', but they *connote* different attitudes, which should be apparent to any reader.

A 'staunch Conservative' and a 'dyed-in-the-wool Tory' are the same person, seen through different eyes, those of approval and those of disapproval. Fog is nasty; mist is rather nice and romantic—yet the denotative difference is actually no more than a mere technicality of definition, a matter of the exact limit of visibility in each case. Examples could be multiplied to show that, in addition to their literal meaning, words often carry implications and suggestions as to the attitude to be adopted to the idea contained in the words.

An illustration of the importance of connotation can be seen by comparing the first stanza of Gray's 'Elegy Written in a Country Churchyard' with a revised version of the same four lines:—

(a) The curfew tolls the knell of parting day,
     The lowing herd wind slowly o'er the lea,
     The ploughman homeward plods his weary way
     And leaves the world to darkness and to me.

(b) The church-bell chimes the ending of the day,
     The mooing cows are strolling o'er the lea
     The ploughman homeward ambles on his way
     And leaves the place to blackness and to me.

The two passages obviously *mean* (i.e. denote) the same thing, but their connotations are clearly different. Each lexical change should be studied closely, and the effect of the change observed.

Practical Cricitism is concerned with connotation, not denotation.

Connotation is, of course, largely subjective. The reader must observe the implications a word has for himself, but sometimes these implications may not be the same as those intended by the poet. When a modern reader comes across

    "Dancing in the chequered shade"

in Milton's 'L'Allegro', he may at once visualise the pattern of light and shadow cast by sunlight through the branches of a tree in terms of the chequered flag of motor racing, or of a chess board, or even of a policeman's cap, none of which associations would have been present in

Milton's mind when he wrote the poem in the seventeenth century. Nevertheless, these ideas may help to clarify the picture conveyed by the word 'chequered'.

On the other hand, the poet may have had an association of ideas that the reader fails to recognise. For example, in Sylvia Plath's poem 'Daddy', on the fourth line there occurs the phrase 'poor and white'. To some people, the association of these two lexical items immediately conjures up ideas of race. The term 'poor white' is often used in a society where racial distinctions, especially colour distinctions, are made. Such a reader, who has recognised the connotation, is thus well prepared for the development of the poem as it deals (among other things) with the German racial policy of Anti-Semitism during the Thirties and Forties.

The best poetry is, of course, very personal to the author, and in a sense can only be fully understood by the author himself. The reader's task must be to become so sensitive to possible connotations that he can go as far as possible towards a complete understanding of the poet's point of view.

A vast number of examples of the importance of connotation can very easily be found. At present we must content ourselves with only a few. In 'Church Going', Larkin ascends the pulpit of an empty church, and imitates the speech of the preacher. He notices that

"the echoes snigger briefly",

not that

"the echoes chuckle briefly".

The difference in connotation should be immediately obvious. In 'The Whitsun Weddings' Larkin refers to porters 'larking with the mails', which is very different from 'playing with the mails'. The same poet, in 'Toads', referring to people who have opted out of conventional society and taken to the nomadic life of the road, says that

"Their *nippers* have got bare feet,

Their unspeakable wives

Are *skinny* as *whippets*".

For the words in italic try substituting 'children',

'thin', and 'greyhounds', and you will at once see how much has been lost.

Thom Gunn, in 'Elvis Presley', refers to the singer '*wielding* a guitar'. 'Wielding' may denote little more than 'holding' or 'playing', but it connotes a great deal more—something of the militancy of modern youth in revolt against conventional society.

The Scottish poet Norman MacCaig, in 'Feeding Ducks', says that a bull 'bugled across five fields', where most writers would have been content with the more normally used 'bellowed'. At once we infer something of the masculinity of the bull when it is given this military connotation.

In 'The Second Coming', Yeats describes the state of chaos which the modern world seems to be approaching. Everything seems to be falling into disintegration, and anarchy is

"   loosed upon the world,
     The blood-dimmed tide is loosed, and everywhere
     The ceremony of innocence is drowned."

Here the denotation of 'loosed' is obvious, but its full connotation—of something powerful and menacing, always present and waiting to break out to destroy mankind,—is brought out by 'tide' and 'drowned', which immediately make us think of the irresistible force of water held in check by a great dam but always threatening, if the dam bursts, to sweep aside and obliterate everything that stands in its path.

These are, of course, only a few random examples of the importance of connotation. The sensitive reader will always be aware of connotation as he reads, and will notice countless other examples for himself. Such a person will not need to be told of the difference between 'casement' and 'window', 'dim' and 'dull', 'breast' and 'chest', and so on. Objectively, the reader must notice the word actually chosen; subjectively, he must then decide what it implies for him.

Closely connected with connotation is the use of *allusion*—an implied reference to some source, in classical mythology, literature, proverb, etc., which the reader is expected to recognise. A full understanding of a poet like Milton, even in a relatively simple poem such as 'L'Allegro', is not possible unless we can recognise allusions to Cerberus, Bacchus, Aurora, Hebe, Hymen, Orpheus, Pluto, and countless other figures of classical mythology. The poet writes on the assumption that his readers, like himself, are thoroughly familiar with these names, which will act like a kind of shorthand, and immediately conjure up in the reader's mind the abstract ideas associated with these concrete figures. Unfortunately this assumption is not true of many modern readers.

The use of literary allusion is not a feature of early poetry only. It exists in all poetry. T. S. Eliot is one of the most important poets of the twentieth century, but throughout almost all of his works there occur references not only to classical mythology but also to literature of all periods and of all languages. Indeed, without a close acquaintance with our literary heritage it is quite impossible to understand fully what Eliot's poetry means. Even in a comparatively simple poem like 'Journey of the Magi' a phrase such as 'three trees on the low sky' means little unless we are familiar with the story of Christ's crucifixion. 'The Waste Land' is a much more complex work, and is quite meaningless in places unless we recognise Eliot's frequent references to and quotations from Shakespeare, Dante, Buddhist literature, and an astonishing variety of other sources.

Even a very contemporary poet such as Philip Larkin is often not fully understood unless we recognise his allusions. Thus in 'Toads' Larkin, bringing out the conflict in many of us between a desire for freedom from the tyranny of work and a desire for security in life, writes,

> "Ah, were I courageous enough
> To shout *Stuff your pension*!
> But I know, all too well, that's the stuff
> That dreams are made on:"

Only those familiar with Shakespeare's 'The Tempest' will grasp the full contrast between the coarse, modern, colloquial expression and the serene acceptance of life

implied in Prospero's lines in Shakespeare's play:—
> "   We are such stuff
> As dreams are made on, and our little life
> Is rounded with a sleep."

Allusions, of course, are not always purely literary. Robert Lowell, in 'Waking in the Blue', describes the first moments in the day of an inmate of a mental hospital. Early in the poem there occurs the line,
> "Absence! My heart grows tense."

Here the allusion is obviously to the proverbial (though originally literary)
> "Absence makes the heart grow fonder."

The use by Lowell of 'tense' will carry no more than its literal meaning to some readers, but to those who recognise the allusion it will have the effect of sudden surprise, contrasting as it does with 'fonder', thus drawing attention to the disordered mental state of such unfortunates.

A totally non-literary allusion can be seen in Larkin's 'The Whitsun Weddings', as he describes the changing landscape as he approaches London by train:—
> "Now fields were building-plots, and poplars cast
> Long shadows over major roads,".

Here the allusion is simply to the road-sign SLOW—MAJOR ROAD AHEAD, and it brings out effectively the growing urbanisation of the scene as the journey approaches its end.

Recognition of allusion always adds a new dimension to our understanding of a poem. Not every reader, of course, will recognise the allusions he comes across. Only through time and extensive reading can we come near to understanding what the poet's intentions are.

AMBIGUITY

Closely related to connotation is the notion of ambiguity, or multiple meaning, which is one of the most striking features of poetry. In ordinary communication, the existstence of several possible interpretations of the same expression would probably be considered a fault. Ambiguity in straightforward expression indicates failure on the part of the writer to make clear exactly what he means. But in poetry the writer often *intends* us to take double or multiple meanings out of the same expression.

Some examples of ambiguity in poetry have already been given. For example, 'Church Going', as we have seen, can mean simply 'going to church', but it can also mean 'the end of the importance of the Church', and both meanings are perfectly acceptable at the same time. Ambiguity is absolutely fundamental to poetry. Indeed, there is a very famous critical work called 'Seven Types of Ambiguity'. Here we must be content with only a few random examples.

Siegfried Sassoon, in 'Memorial Tablet', writing ironically of the blood-shed of the First World War, says,

"Two bleeding years I fought in France for Squire."
Here, 'bleeding' has two acceptable and approriate meanings—that war was literally a bleeding experience for those who suffered in it, but it was also 'bleeding'— at the very mildest—in the colloquial vocabulary of the soldier who took part, even if the word here carries no connotations of bloodshed at all. It is entirely right that a poem written in the persona of a front-line soldier should contain some of the vocabulary of such a man, but something extra is added when the word chosen includes a second and equally appropriate meaning.

Writing of the Second World War in 'Naming of Parts', Henry Reed describes the process of 'easing the spring' of a rifle by sliding the bolt rapidly backwards and forwards. But almost immediately afterwards he talks of bees and flowers and the beauty of Nature in general, and calls it 'easing the Spring'. The ambiguity is seen at once in the use of the capital letter in this instance. By using virtually the same phrase in these two totally different senses, the poet brings out sharply the conflict between the attitudes imposed by war and those held by sensitive men in times of peace. The same point is well brought at the end of the poem by the use of ambiguity. One of the 'parts' of the rifle which the recruits have been learning is the 'point of balance'— the point on the rifle at which the whole weapon can be balanced easily even on one finger. In the last stanza Reed refers to

"   the point of balance,
Which in our case we have not got;"
an ambiguous reference, not only to the shortage of
equipment in the army at the time, but also to a short-
coming in society as a whole, which by the very act of
going to war has lost its 'point of balance'.

Sylvia Plath's poem 'Daddy' is a very powerful and
disturbing work concerning, among other things, the
final rejection of a false, childish impression of her father
as some kind of heroic figure. It is an American poem,
and British readers may fail to notice the ambiguity
contained in the line
"So daddy, I'm finally through",
repeated more emphatically in the last line of the poem:—
"Daddy, daddy, you bastard, I'm through."
'I'm through' in modern American can have two distinct
meanings. 'You're through' is what the telephone
operator says when she has established the connection
which the caller has asked for. Thus the poet may be
saying, 'I have established a connection—I am in touch
with the truth—I am no longer deceived.' This meaning
is shown to be acceptable by an immediate reference in
the poem to 'the black telephone'. But when an American
other than a telephone operator says 'I'm through', he
often means 'I'm finished—it's all over—I am bringing
the whole affair to an end.' That this second meaning
of the words is also acceptable is all too sadly suggested
by the fact that not long after writing it the poet com-
mitted suicide.

Another example occurs in David Holbrook's 'Unholy
Marriage', which is concerned with a young couple on a
motor-bike being killed by crashing at high speed into
the rear of a stationary lorry. The accident happens
"Before he could think, Christ!"
Again, the ambiguity is deliberate. The young driver's
last thought in life was either a prayer, or a profanity—
or both in the same instant. Only poetry, by its use of
ambiguity, can so demonstrate in the smallest possible
number of words the complexity and contradictory
nature of some of our deepest emotions.

So far, ambiguity has been dealt with as a purely

verbal matter—that is, that one word may be capable of being understood in several different ways. There is a very important sub-division of ambiguity which is more than simply verbal. The same event or experience of the poet is seen to have more than one *value* to him. This is sometimes called *Ambivalence*. We say that the poet expresses 'an ambivalent attitude' to the experience. The use of the two terms, ambiguity and ambivalence, is perhaps an unnecessary refinement, however, and it may be that for most students the one general term, ambiguity, will prove sufficient. For those who can see the difference, two examples of ambivalence will be given.

Yeats's poem 'Easter 1916' contains—on three separate occasions—the line 'A *terrible beauty* is born'. This highly unusual combination of words is an expression of an ambivalent attitude to the Rising—the bloodshed is terrible, but the noble self-sacrifice is beautiful. This ambivalence is continued later in the poem in a passage which deals with 'stone'. First we have some lines which suggest the eternal 'monumental' nature of stone—the stone which is 'erected in memory' of some great hero. But then the poet says,

"Too long a sacrifice
Can make a stone of the heart."

The close association of 'stone' and 'heart' must immediately make us think of hard inhumanity, whereas previously 'stone' has been used to suggest heroism and self-sacrifice. In this way the poet is able to indicate his ambivalent attitude to the Irish Rising.

The second example is taken from Ted Hughes's 'Thrushes', in which he comments on the ability of the thrush to concentrate on one single purpose in life—to kill and eat. In the second stanza, Hughes notes the same single-mindedness in two vastly different examples:—

" Mozart's brain had it, and the shark's mouth
That hungers down the blood-smell even to a leak
of its own
Side and devouring of itself:"

The equation of Mozart's skill in music with the cannibalistic ruthlessness of the shark tracking down blood, by its very incongruity, reveals the poet's ambivalent attitude to the single-minded.   Such conduct can be wholly admirable, he is saying, but at the same time it can also be wholly detestable.

COLLOCATION

An important concept in discussing poetry is that of collocation—the way in which words tend to appear beside, or very close to, other words which are closely associated in idea with the original words.   Thus we would expect the word 'green' to collocate with 'grass', 'lawn', 'young', 'Celtic', 'envy', 'eyes', and many more—but not with 'electricity', or 'orchestra', or 'technological'. Similarly, the word 'ass', might occur in close proximity to 'silly', 'frightful', 'ox', or 'bray', but we would be surprised to find it in collocation with 'experiment', 'hooligan', 'midnight', or 'leisure'.

One of the special attractions of poetry—and one which must be of interest to the exponent of Practical Criticism— is the use by the poet of collocations which are startling in their unexpectedness.   The seventeenth century poet, Andrew Marvell, has a poem entitled 'Thoughts in a Garden'.   We shall not be surprised in a poem with this title to find the word 'green' occurring.   'Green' and 'garden' are obviously conventional collocations.   But what is the effect of a couplet such as this?

"Annihilating all that's made
To a green thought in a green shade."?

'Green' simply does not collocate with 'thought' or with 'shade', yet here the poet places the words together.   By doing so, he concentrates our attention on them, and succeeds in conveying the almost overpowering effect of the beauty of growing things.   Whenever such an unusual collocation occurs its effect is striking, and having been struck by it the reader must then try to appreciate all the implications of the surprising collocation.

Examples of this are innumerable, because unexpected collocation of words is possibly the most striking single feature that distinguishes poetry from other forms of communication.   This is not a modern device.   It has existed as long as poetry has existed.   Shakespeare tells us that

"Macbeth hath *murdered sleep*"
and that
"Parting is such *sweet sorrow*."
Milton, in 'Lycidas', bitterly condemns the false pastors of the Church who care little for the welfare of their flock, in the lines

"Blind mouths! that scarce themselves know how to
hold
A sheep-hook".

Yeats, in 'Easter 1916', indicates his ambivalent attitude to the Rising in Ireland in 1916—hatred of violence, yet respect for the exponents of violence—in the repeated phrase

"A terrible beauty is born".

Dylan Thomas, in 'Fern Hill', tries to recapture some of the excitement of childhood with unexpected collocations such as

"and happy as the grass was green"
"and once below a time"
"all the sun long"
"all the moon long"
"happy as the heart was long"
"in the lamb white days".

Ted Hughes, in 'Wind', brings out the powerful force of the wind, upsetting all normal movement, in the line,

"At noon I *scaled* along the house side"

Larkin, in 'Church Going', imagines a time when no one will enter a church to worship, and the only person interested in such a building will be

"Some ruin-*bibber*, *randy* for antique,
Or Christmas-*addict*".

The same poet, in 'The Whitsun Weddings', talks of the older women among the wedding parties who "shared the secret like a *happy funeral*", bringing into sharp contrast the simple joy of wedding festivities with something of the hard, and even painful, realities of marriage.

Examples of unexpected collocation could be multiplied indefinitely, but pointlessly. This is the stuff of which poetry is made, and without it there is no poetry. Whenever an unusual collocation occurs, it ought to strike the reader immediately and force him to some consideration of the implications of the collocation.

IMAGERY

'Imagery' is a term which is difficult to describe with precision, because it is often used very loosely. Broadly speaking, it can be applied to any writing which is descriptive, anything which helps the reader to visualise a scene and so to experience the poet's experience. The term is often extended to include an appeal to any of the senses, not just that of sight. Aural imagery, for example, appeals to the sense of hearing, just as visual imagery appeals to the sense of seeing. Here we shall be concerned only with visual imagery. Aural imagery will be glanced at when we deal with sound effects in poetry.

Any kind of descriptive writing involves imagery—the description of a storm in 'Tam o' Shanter', Wordsworth's description of "a host of golden daffodils". In such simple descriptive writing, the effectiveness of the imagery is to be judged by each reader for himself, by asking how real the scene appears to him as a result of the poet's words. Consider the following stanza from Philip Larkin's 'The Whitsun Weddings':—

"All afternoon, through the tall heat that slept
    For miles inland,
A slow and stopping curve southwards we kept.
Wide farms went by, short-shadowed cattle, and
Canals with floatings of industrial froth;
A hothouse flashed, uniquely; hedges dipped
And rose; and now and then a smell of grass
Displaced the reek of buttoned carriage-cloth
Until the next town, new and nondescript,
Approached with acres of dismantled cars."

Here Larkin presents us with a series of pictures which are vivid in our minds because we have all shared the experience of travelling by train through the countryside on a hot afternoon. We recognise the experience, but only the poet's skill can re-create it for us. Instead of commenting on the imagery, perhaps it would be better to pose a series of questions, which the reader can answer for himself:—

What does he mean by 'tall heat'?

How can heat sleep?

What is 'a slow and stopping curve'?

What is conveyed by 'wide farms went by'?

What are 'short-shadowed cattle'?

Can you visualise 'floatings of industrial froth'?

What is the effect of 'uniquely'?

From what viewpoint do the hedges dip and rise?

Do you recognise from your own experience 'the reek of buttoned carriage-cloth'?

Did the next town *literally* approach?

Does 'with acres of dismantled cars' seem an accurate description of the outskirts of a town approached by rail?

This poem is an excellent example of imagery used to great effect in re-creating a scene which the reader will recognise, before the poet makes his comment on what he has observed.

Imagery, however, has an importance far beyond that of simple description of a scene. Often a poet, in order to describe one thing, will resort to imagery which suggests something else. Ted Hughes, for example, begins his poem 'Wind' with the line

"This house has been far out at sea all night".

To convey the sense of fear aroused by the storm, Hughes has used the image of the sea, with all the connotations of fear that 'far out at sea' carries for us.

Imagery often depends for its success on this emotive power that some words have to connote more than they denote. Very often we recognise such imagery by the fact that 'sets' of words occur—a series of words connected with colour, or death, or war, or the sea, or religion, and so on. The early stanzas of 'The Whitsun Weddings' are highly descriptive, as we have seen. But a new type of imagery arises towards the end, and it no longer merely describes the scene. As London is approached, Larkin thinks of

"Its postal districts packed *like squares of wheat*".

This idea of growth, harvest, fruitfulness is continued throughout the last stanza in phrases such as 'ready to be loosed', 'power', 'swelled', 'an arrow-shower', and 'somewhere becoming rain'. The image of fruitfulness, contrasting sharply as it does with the cold, dry, even arrogant attitude of the detached observer in the earlier part of the poem, is surely what the whole poem is about. No matter how superior the poet may seem to be in his ridicule of the working-class wedding-parties, he comes at last to recognise the supremacy of the life-giving force that all these new marriages represent.

Another good example occurs in 'A Peasant', by R. S. Thomas. Here again the poet skilfully uses imagery of the simple kind to paint an accurate picture, which we can visualise, of the crude, ugly, and even repulsive peasant of the Welsh hills. Having stirred us to a feeling almost of disgust at this creature, he ends with the following lines:—

"Yet this is your prototype, who, season by season
Against siege of rain and the wind's attrition,
Preserves his stock, an impregnable fortress
Not to be stormed even in death's confusion.
Remember him then, for he, too, is a winner of wars,
Enduring like a tree under the curious stars."

Here we should notice 'siege', attrition', 'an impregnable fortress', 'to be stormed'—a set of words connected with war, showing that, despite his apparently repulsive features, there is something heroic in this man's powers of endurance against all that nature can do to him, for 'he, too, is a winner of wars'.

Ted Hughes's poem 'Thrushes' has already been referred to several times. Surely something is added to our understanding of the poem when we notice 'coiled steel', 'triggered', 'a stab', 'nothing but bounce and stab', 'this bullet and automatic purpose'—imagery which conveys effectively the lethal and unfeeling quality of this apparently delicate creature.

The most condensed form of imagery is to be found in figures of speech. Not all of the so-called figures of speech involve visual imagery, however. Alliteration, for example, is a matter of sound effect. Others, such as antithesis and anti-climax, are matters of arrangement of ideas. Thus when Gray says,

"The paths of glory lead but to the grave",

he is using alliteration to give emphasis to the antithesis, but he is not using imagery. The anti-climax in Eliot's 'Journey of the Magi', when all of the wearisome details of the difficulties of the journey are concluded by the arrival at the stable in Bethlehem, and "it was (you may say) satisfactory" is very striking, but no imagery is involved. When we read in 'The Whitsun Weddings' that "the last confetti and advice were thrown" we notice the incongruity, but this again is a matter of word arrangement rather than of imagery.

Metaphor and simile, however, when they are well used, represent imagery at its most concise, giving that sudden pictorial flash which can convey as much in a word as several whole sentences of non-figurative language. Presumably 'metaphor' and 'simile' are already familiar terms. All that is required is a few examples of their effective use.

Consider T. S. Eliot, in 'The Love Song of J. Alfred Prufrock', who sums up a whole life spent in useless triviality with

"I have measured out my life with coffee spoons."

For all their smallness, there is something strong and vigorous associated with tea-spoons; soup spoons suggest solid sustenance; but coffee spoons—as distinct from tea spoons used for stirring coffee—convey only the empty ceremonial of the polite social gathering, where coffee is taken in tiny fragile cups in quantities which can slake no thirst. What could be more trivial than coffee spoons? Thus the whole uselessness of the empty life he has led is revealed. Most people think of 'milestones' in their lives; Prufrock's milestones are coffee spoons!

Ted Hughes, in one phrase, 'nostrils a surface bead', presents an immediate picture of the otter and conveys something of its mystery—the paradox of a creature clumsy on land, completely at home in water, yet utterly dependent on air for survival. His only connection with our world is reduced to one tiny bead on the surface of the water, but without this 'bead' life is not possible for him.

Effectiveness is, in the end, a matter for individual judgment. Consider the following examples of metaphor and simile, all taken from Ted Hughes, and decide how effective they are.

"The tent of the hills drummed and strained its guyrope" ('Wind')
"Daylong this tomcat lies stretched flat
As an old rough mat." ('Esther's Tomcat')
"Like a bundle of old rope and iron
Sleeps till blue dusk." ('Esther's Tomcat')
"Green tigering the gold." ('Pike')

An extreme form of imagery is to be found in the use of *symbolism*, in which an image represents something visual, but also often a vast number of other ideas which the poet associates with the word. Yeats and Eliot are two poets in whom words often have strong symbolic meanings. In Yeats, there are always special meanings—almost like a private code—attached to the image of the swan, the tower, or the staircase, for example. In Eliot, the garden or the desert or the sea can represent far more than they may seem to. In such cases, full understanding of the poet's meaning is not possible unless we have some private knowledge—not revealed simply by a study of the words of the poem—of what the poet intends the symbols to stand for. This is a vast field of study, but—perhaps fortunately—it has no relevance to Practical Criticism at the present level of discussion.

One final example of effective imagery may now be given. In 'The Second Coming', Yeats seeks to convey all his fears about the anarchic state of society and the impending change which, he feels, must occur if order is to be restored to chaos:—

"The Second Coming! Hardly are those words out
When a vast image out of *Spiritus Mundi*
Troubles my sight: somewhere in sands of the desert
A shape with lion body and the head of a man,
A gaze blank and pitiless as the sun,
Is moving its slow thighs, while all about it
Reel shadows of the indignant desert birds."

5   Sound Patterns

Some reference has already been made to ways in which sound and meaning are interrelated. In this chapter we shall consider sound effects rather more systematically, but not exhaustively. There are, unfortunately, some serious difficulties in connection with sound effects. We may theorise as much as we like about vowel sounds, but we must remember that pronunciation varies enormously over the different regions of the English-speaking world. A poem written by an Australian will sound quite differently from its Australian reading if it is read aloud by a Londoner, a Yorkshireman, a Glaswegian, an Aberdonian, a Welshman, a Bostonian, a 'deep south' American, a Dubliner, or a Jamaican— yet all are native speakers of English. Anything that is said about pronunciation, therefore, must be treated with reservations. Similarly, intonation is obviously of great importance, but intonation, like pronunciation, varies enormously from region to region, and this makes it difficult to be dogmatic about the correct intonation to be used in any poem.

The ideal reader of a poem ought to be the poet himself, because only he knows the precise sound effects which he intended to produce in his poem. Nowadays public recitals by poets are very much in vogue, and countless recordings exist of poets reading their own works. But the talents required to be a good poet are not the same as the talents required to be a good reader, and some good poets are unquestionably bad readers. It is sometimes maintained that the best reader of poetry is a good actor, and many fine recordings of poems have been made by actors. But in his reading there can be no certainty that the actor has not used his skill to convey an interpretation quite different from that intended by the poet. It is, in fact, impossible to say what is the 'correct' reading of any poem.

This chapter, therefore, will deal with only a few of the most obvious ways in which sound can contribute to the total meaning of a poem.

Most poetry in English is based on rhythmical patterns. Such patterns exist in all utterances, but in poetry some kind of regularity is often imposed on the patterns. For convenience it is necessary to use some technical terms in talking of these patterns, but it must be stressed that there is no merit in simply knowing the technical names for the patterns which can be recognised, unless we are aware of the effectiveness of the patterns which the poet has chosen.

All utterances consist of a series of syllables, some of which are stressed and some unstressed. This can be indicated by the use of the symbols u for an unstressed syllable and x for a stressed syllable. Thus the sound of the word 'tomorrow' could be indicated by

        u   x   u
        tomorrow,
while 'today' would appear as
        u x
        today.
            x   u u
The word 'invalid' is a noun which means 'a sick person',
            u   x u
whereas the word 'invalid' is an adjective which means 'not valid'. A few well known book titles might have their stresses indicated as follows:—

        u   x   u   x   u   x   u   x
        A Book of Verse for Boys and Girls

        u   x u   x u u
        The Golden Treasury

        u   x   xu u
        The New Poetry

        u   x   u   x u   u x   u u u   x
        The Penguin Book of Contemporary Verse
In poetry there are four basic patterns:—

    (a) *Iambic rhythm*
        u x   u x u x
        I want/to buy/a car
Each 'foot' consists of ux—that is, an unstressed syllable followed by a stressed syllable.

(b) *Trochaic rhythm*

```
x u  x  u   x   u  x u
```
Fifty/ways of/making/money

Each foot consists of a stressed syllable followed by an unstressed syllable.

(c) *Anapaestic rhythm*

```
u  u  x   u u   x  u  u  x
```
If you want/to have fun/at the fair

Each foot consists of two unstressed syllables followed by one stressed syllable.

(d) *Dactylic rhythm*

```
x  u  u  x u   u   x  u   u
```
Flying a/flag on the/battlements

Each foot consists of a stressed syllable followed by two unstressed syllables.

Of these four basic patterns, by far the most common in English poetry is the iambic. So common is it, in fact, that its presence need never be discussed, only its absence. Whenever a poet chooses anything other than iambic rhythm we should ask ourselves why he has done so, and how successful his choice has been. The most frequent variation is the use of anapaestic rhythm, which is particularly effective in suggesting great speed. Gray's 'Elegy', for example, is written in conventional iambic feet, entirely appropriate for a poem reflecting on the subject of death. On the other hand, the whole purpose of Browning's 'How they Brought the Good News from Ghent to Aix' is to convey the breathless excitement of a race against time in some situation where speed is a matter of life or death. Appropriately, Browning chose to write in anapaests, a rhythm which conveys perfectly the hoofbeats of the galloping horses:—

> "Not a word to each other; we kept the great pace
> Neck by neck, stride by stride, never changing our
> place;".

Read these lines aloud, and contrast the sound effect with that of the following much slower—iambic—version:—

> "We said no word, we kept the pace,
> Rode neck by neck, not changing place".

The trochee and the dactyl are inverted forms of the

iamb and the anapaest, with the stress coming at the beginning of each foot instead of at the end. They are much less frequently used, and generally their purpose is to give some additional solemnity and grandeur to the occasion. Thus Longfellow, telling the story of Hiawatha, writes in trochaic rhythm to suggest that his story is that not just of one man but of a whole tribe. Tennyson, in 'The Charge of the Light Brigade', like Browning in 'The Good News', depicts the speed of a group of horsemen, but adopts dactylic instead of anapaestic rhythm as being more appropriate for a poem celebrating an action of great gallantry but ending in terrible slaughter:—

"When can their glory fade?
O the wild charge they made!
    All the world wondered.
Honour the charge they made!
Honour the Light Brigade,
    Noble six hundred!"

So far we have considered the four most common rhythms in English poetry. In a great deal of poetry—but not all—we find that the poet has adopted one of these patterns and retained it, with minor modifications, throughout the poem. In such poetry, written in a regularly-recurring rhythmical pattern, we usually find also that the number of feet in each line is also based on a regular pattern—all lines consisting of five feet, for example, or lines of four feet alternating with lines of three feet. For sheer convenience it is advisable to know the names given for lines of different lengths—though once again it must be stressed that these technical terms are used as a matter of convenience only. The technical terms of poetry should never be regarded as a body of knowledge worthwhile for its own sake. What matters is that we should recognise the significance of what the poet has done, not that we should know the name for it.

It is theoretically possible for a line of poetry to contain almost any number of feet, but in practice only the following need be known by name:—

Hexameter	—	6 feet (rare)
Pentameter	—	5 feet
Tetrameter	—	4 feet

Trimeter   —   3 feet
Dimeter   —   2 feet (rare)

Of these, by far the most common is the pentameter. It might almost be said, in fact, that iambic pentameter is the basic line in English poetry. If a poet chooses to write in a regular pattern, then he will normally choose to write in pentameter, and when he adopts a longer or a shorter line we should be immediately interested. Once again we may take Gray's 'Elegy' as the 'norm', since it is written in iambic pentameter:—

"The curfew tolls the knell of parting day,
The lowing herd wind slowly o'er the lea,
The ploughman homeward plods his weary way,
And leaves the world to darkness and to me."

If this slow, steady rhythm is suitable for Gray's reflections on death, it can hardly also be suitable for such a brisk, humorous poem as Burns's 'Tam o' Shanter'. In fact, Burns writes his poem in iambic tetrameter, and the shorter line produces a sound effect much more in keeping with the tone of his poem. He still retains the iambic form, however. He might have chosen to write in anapaests for purposes of speed, especially in the chase by the witches, but the anapaestic rhythm would not have been appropriate for some of the slower-moving passages of the poem. In fact the form he adopted matches perfectly the content, and, as we shall see later, he is able, within the iambic tetrameter, both to slow down the movement and to give an additional impression of speed where it is most appropriate.

Just as the short tetrameter is useful in suggesting speed, so the long hexameter can be useful in suggesting slowness and weariness, particularly if one hexameter is used after a succession of pentameters. In 'The Cotter's Saturday Night', Burns writes in pentameters, but ends each stanza with a hexameter. In most cases the use of the hexameter has no particular connection with the meaning of the line, but at the end of the second stanza it is very effective as he describes the slow, weary walk of a man returning home at the end of a long, hard day's work:—

"And weary o'er the moor his course does hameward
                     bend."

Alexander Pope disapproved of hexameters—called Alexandrines—used for no good reason, and brilliantly conveys their long-drawn-out effect by using one himself:—

"A needless Alexandrine ends the song,
Which, like a wounded snake, drags its slow length
along."

What has been said so far is no more than a very sketchy outline of the fundamentals of rhythm patterns. Probably it has been familiar ground to most readers. The regular patterns described can be very important, but poetry—especially modern poetry—is less concerned with patterns for their own sake than with the effect produced when stress serves to draw attention to an expression of particular importance. Regularity is no longer seen as a virtue in itself. Nowadays, when a poet adopts a regular form we ask why he has done so, whereas in the past a regular form was taken for granted, and a departure from regularity would have provoked such a question.

Modern poetry often seems to employ not only the vocabulary but also the rhythm of ordinary speech. Thus it becomes all the more striking when the reader notices that somehow the poet has contrived to make certain words stand out because of the stress they have been given. For example, in Eliot's 'Journey of the Magi', we read first of the hardships of the early part of the journey these men made to Bethlehem. Then as they come nearer to their objective there is a change:—

"Then at dawn we came down to a temperate valley,
Wet, below the snow line, smelling of vegetation;
With a running stream and a water-mill beating the
darkness,
And three trees on the low sky".

This last line stands out from the rest first of all because it is so much shorter than the others. Some additional emphasis is given by the use of rhyme in 'three trees'. But what makes it stand out most of all is the unusual pattern of stresses:—

u   x   x u u x   x
"And three trees on the low sky"

All the emphasis is placed on 'three trees' and 'low sky' and an immediate picture strikes us. The words thus emphasised make us pause, and soon we realise that something more than a mere picture is involved. At this moment of Christ's birth we are suddenly given an image of his future crucifixion as one of three on the hill of Calvary. This image of Death together with Birth becomes the central idea of the poem as we read on from this point. Had the poet not attracted our attention by placing strongly stressed words side by side, we might have missed the significance of his allusion.

ONOMATOPOEIA

Probably the most obvious of all sound effects is the device known as onomatopoeia—the use of words whose sound suggests their meaning. The most simple examples are words which are the names given to actual sounds. A bell 'rings', and the word sounds like the sound of the bell. But there can be bells of many different kinds. Some bells 'tinkle', some 'clang', and others 'boom'. There should be no difficulty in identifying what kind of bell is referred to in each case—the words themselves tell us. One man may speak in a low 'rumble', whereas another may speak in a high-pitched 'squeak'. The 'crack' of the pistol shot is a very different sound from the 'thud' of the boxer's gloved fist striking his opponent's body.

It is easy, of course, to identify these obvious examples of onomatopoeia, but it is less easy—and more important —to be aware of *how* the different effects are produced. The sounds of both consonants and vowels must be considered.

The different consonant sounds can be classified in many ways, but for our purposes there is one basic distinction to be made. Some consonants, called 'plosives', are instantaneous in their sound. The organs of speech— lips, teeth, tongue—are put into the right place, the supply of air from the lungs is deliberately held back, and then it is suddenly released, producing sounds such as 'p' and 'b', 't' and 'd', 'k' and 'g' (as in 'gas'). Other consonants, which go under a variety of names, are produced by an emission of breath which is not instantaneous, but which can last as long as the speaker desires—sounds like 'l', 's', 'z', 'f', and 'v'. The plosive sounds can be very effective in suggesting something sudden, and also something ugly and unpleasant. On the other hand, a preponderance of non-plosive consonants can suggest something more long-drawn-out, often with a marked soothing effect. Not all of such consonants have the same effect, however. We may notice a soporific effect produced by a succession of 'm' and 'l' sounds, whereas there may be something more alert—and even unpleasantly so—in the serpent-like quality produced by a succession of 's' sounds.

Consider now two words 'crack' and 'splash'. The first word begins and ends with the same plosive 'k' sound, and the sound produced accurately suggests the meaning of the word. The sound associated with 'splash', however, is quite different, and the difference is conveyed by the use of 's' at the beginning and 'sh' at the end—both sounds which are more long-drawn-out than the plosives. It might be interesting to imagine that the word 'splash' does not exist, and we are seeking a word to convey all that is meant by 'splash'. What about 'splass'? Sound the two words, and you will hear a difference. 'Splass' seems to cut through the water too efficiently, with none of the turbulent spray thrown up when we 'splash' into the water. Why not 'slash', then? This time we miss the plosive sound of 'p', which suggests the very instant when the body makes contact with the water. If we must have this moment of impact, what is wrong with 'spash'? Again, sound the two words and listen for the difference. The plosive sound is necessary, but if it is followed at once by the vowel we are given the impression of a highly efficient diver entering the water and cutting through it like a blade, whereas what is required is the sound of a body entering the water rather clumsily and meeting resistance, and this impression is conveyed by the addition of the 'l' sound.

Like consonants, vowels can be divided into two broad classifications—front vowels and back vowels. Front vowels are produced towards the front of the mouth, back vowels towards the back. The best way to learn the distinction is to pronounce a succession of words, stopping each time to consider exactly how the tongue is placed to sound each vowel. Try the following list:—

    beat
    bit
    bet
    bat
    Bart
    bot
    bought
    boat
    boot

Then try sounding the *vowels only* in quick succession, all in one breath, noticing what happens to the tongue and the jaw as you make the different sounds. The sounds produced at the start are front vowels, and the sounds produced towards the end are back vowels. When a writer wants to suggest lightness and speed, he will use front vowels; when he wants to suggest a slow solemnity he will look for words which use back vowels.

Consider the difference, both in sound and in meaning, between 'quick' and 'slow'. Part of the difference in sound is produced by the use of the instantaneous plosive consonant 'k' at the end of 'quick'. But 'quick' is a much 'speedier' word than 'quake', yet the final consonant is the same. The difference lies in the vowel sound. The front vowel 'i' suggests a speed not found in the vowel sound of 'quake'. When we combine the effect of plosive consonants and front vowel in 'quick' and contrast it with the non-plosive consonants and back vowel of 'slow' we realise at once how different is the effect of each word.

A good illustration of the skilful selection of vowel sounds can be found in Milton's companion pieces, 'L'Allegro' and 'Il Penseroso'. Here the poet represents two sharply contrasting attitudes to life—the gay, lively sociable man contrasted with the man who finds his pleasure more in silence, solitude, and study than in joviality. In order to make the contrast more obvious, Milton adopted identical forms for both poems, and since happiness was the theme common to both he chose to write in couplets of iambic tetrameter. But while the lively metre of 'Tam o' Shanter' is perfectly suitable for 'L'Allegro', it might seem quite out of place in 'Il Penseroso', although Milton's purpose demands that both poems be written in the same form. He found the solution in his vowel sounds. 'L'Allegro' relies heavily on front vowels in its stressed syllables, whereas 'Il Penseroso' tends towards back vowels. You will at once hear the difference if you try reading the following passages aloud:—

'*L'Allegro*'
"Haste thee, Nymph, and bring with thee
Jest and youthful jollity,
Quips, and cranks, and wanton wiles
Nods, and becks, and wreathed smiles."

'*Il Penseroso*'
"Come, pensive nun, devout and pure,
Sober, steadfast, and demure,
All in a robe of darkest grain
Flowing with majestic train."

Here we have two poems, apparently identical in form, yet one is brisk and lively, the other slow and solemn. The different effects are produced by the choice of words, in one poem using a preponderance of front vowels and in the other a preponderance of back vowels.

A similar example occurs in Tennyson's 'Morte d'Arthur'. Three times Sir Bedivere sets out to throw the sword Excalibur back into the lake from which it originally and mysteriously came. This is a task which he finds extremely distasteful, and on the first and second occasions he is unable to carry out the king's command. After his first failure we have,
"So strode he back slow to the wounded king."
The second failure ends with
"And so strode back slow to the wounded king."
But at the third attempt he is determined to carry out his instructions, and refuses to stop even for an instant to reconsider the matter. Everything is done in great haste, the sword is thrown into the lake,
"And lightly went the other to the king".
If these three lines are read in succession, the totally

different sound of the third version will be immediately apparent, and the difference will be easily traced to the use of front vowels in the stressed syllables.

A few other examples of onomatopoeia in use in poetry must now suffice to finish this section. Tennyson's 'The Brook' is full of onomatopoeia of the simple kind—that which suggests an actual sound. Thus we have:—

"I bubble into eddying bays,
I babble on the pebbles."

Compare this with Larkin in 'The Whitsun Weddings':—

"The river's level drifting breadth began."

Both poets are describing the movement of a water-way—the one a quickly-moving small stream moving downhill over a stony bed, the other a broad river moving slowly over almost flat countryside. The quick movement of the former is accentuated by the frequent use of the plosive 'b' and the liquid 'l' sound, and by the near-rhyme of 'bubble', 'babble', and 'pebbles', whereas Larkin conveys the effect of the broad, slow river by a much subtler form of onomatopoeia, in which many devices are combined. There is an unusual nominal group, a headword (breadth) preceded by three modifiers; there is an unexpected lexical choice—'breadth' began, not 'course'; the words 'level' and 'drifting' are both onomatopoeic, since each suggests by its sound a slow kind of movement.

A totally different sound effect is produced by Larkin in 'Church Going':—

"I step inside, letting the door thud shut."

Both 'thud' and 'shut', by their vowel sounds and by their final plosive sound, convey perfectly the actual sound made by the heavy door of the church. Some of Larkin's verbal skill can be seen if we try to improve on these words:—

"Letting the door slam shut
                    bang shut
                    slam to
                    crash closed

In each case, the sound effect is clearly wrong. Perhaps some reader may be able to produce something better than Larkin—certainly the attempt to do so will teach us a great deal about the art of the poet.

Another good example is to be found in Ted Hughes's 'An Otter', which he describes as

"Walloping up roads with the milk wagon".

We are struck at once by the incongruity of the otter sharing the early-morning roadway with the very urban milkwagon. Then we observe the surprising lexical choice of 'walloping' instead of a word like 'journeying' or 'travelling'. Finally, we observe the onomatopoeic effect of this ungainly word, so perfectly chosen to suggest the ungainly movement of a creature of land which is more at home in water than on land.

Not only sound and movement can be suggested by onomatopoeia. Anything that is beautiful can be suggested by beautiful sounds; anything that is ugly can be suggested by ugly sounds. John Masefield's poem 'Cargoes' has already been referred to. There is something remote, romantic and beautiful in

"Quinquireme of Nineveh from distant Ophir",
and in

"Stately Spanish galleon coming from the Isthmus".
But an entirely different impression is conveyed by the sheer ugliness of sound in

"Dirty British coaster with a salt-caked smoke stack."
Here the ugliness is conveyed by the frequency of plosive sounds—d, t, b, t, c, t, t, c, k, d, k, t, ck. The harshness is especially brought out by the fact that twice we have two plosive sounds coming together, in the 't' and 'c' and 'k' and' d' of 'salt-caked'—a most difficult combination of sounds to pronounce.

Something similar can be observed in Burns's 'Tam o' Shanter', a brisk, free-flowing poem if ever there was one. But then we come to the devil in the shape of

"A towsy tyke, black, grim and large".
Again we have several plosives, but especially we have two coming together in 'black, grim'. The presence of these two plosive sounds together—even without the presence of the comma—forces us to pause in our reading, and to alter the stress which we place on the words. The basic rhythm of the poem, as we have seen, is iambic tetrameter, but it is quite impossible to read this

line aloud with the same rhythm as that which we would give to

"When chapman billies leave the street"

or

"But pleasures are like poppies spread".

If we read all three lines aloud, we must at once notice how different is the effect produced by

"A towsy tyke, black, grim and large",

and we must at once observe how successful this rather ugly-sounding line is in suggesting a picture of the prince of evil.

ALLITERATION

Closely allied to onomatopoeia is the device known as alliteration—the use of a succession of identical consonant sounds, usually but not always at the beginning of successive words. A good example is seen in the 'b' and 'l' sounds of

"I bubble into eddying bays,
I babble on the pebbles."

This is a good illustration of alliteration used for purposes of onomatopoeia. Another well-known example occurs in the first stanza of Gray's 'Elegy':—

"The ploughman homeward plods his weary way."

Compare 'ploughman plods' with 'farmer walks', and immediately you will notice the loss in sound effect. One is a mere statement of what happens, whereas the other seeks to convey by its sound the heavy tread of the tired man, his big boots, the muddy ground, the dull routine of the whole operation. Again, 'weary way' is quite different from 'tired path'. The use of the long-drawn-out 'w' is more effective in suggesting exhaustion than the instantaneous effect of plosives such as 't' and 'p'.

Apart from onomatopoeic purposes, alliteration serves to draw attention to anything which is particularly important, especially where there is some sharp contrast. Thomas Gray in his 'Elegy' says

"The paths of glory lead but to the grave".

He could have said

"The paths of glory lead but to the tomb"

or

"The roads of glory lead but to the grave",

but the contrast between the greatness of a particular man's life and the end which he will share with all men is brought out more effectively when our attention is drawn to it by the alliteration of 'glory' and 'grave'.

Onomatopoeia and contrast are the most profitable uses of alliteration. Sometimes, however, it can be used simply for our amusement. Thus in 'Toads' Philip Larkin, talking of the desire that many feel to be freed from the obligations of a steady, secure job, says that

"Lots of men live on their wits."

At this point we may not notice the alliteration contained in 'lots' and 'live'. But then he goes on to give examples:—

"Lecturers, lispers,
Losels, loblolly-men, louts—"

The use of alliteration combines with his very unusual lexical choice to produce an effect verging on absurdity. We understand 'louts', but are struck by the strange idea that lecturers, whom we tend to respect, are regarded as men who live on their wits. Then we wonder just what is meant by lispers, losels, and loblolly-men, and by the time we find out we realise that the words have been used merely to amuse us.

The effect of alliteration is always to give emphasis and make a phrase memorable—a fact well known to the composers of advertising material, with their slogans such as 'Guinness is good for you', and 'McEwan's is the best buy in beer'. Whenever we recognise alliteration in poetry, we should try to find out why the phrase has been singled out for this special emphasis. Effective alliteration is not a merely decorative trick of style; it is a device for attracting the reader's attention to something which the poet considers important.

RHYME

The function of rhyme is essentially the same as that of alliteration—to attract the reader's attention to something

of importance by the recurring use of similar sounds—
but whereas alliteration is concerned with consonants
rhyme is concerned either with vowels alone or with
vowels and the consonants which follow them.

Straight away we must discard all ideas of learning
off well-known 'rhyme schemes'—things like ballad
rhyme, the Burns stanza, the Petrarchan sonnet, the
Shakespearean sonnet, the Spenserian stanza, and so on.
The mere naming of a rhyme scheme is of no value
unless we can relate the form to the content. Students
of Shakespeare's sonnets, for example, should notice the
rhyme scheme,

a b a b   c d c d   e f e f   g g.

But merely to notice this is worthless unless we also
observe that the last two lines—the only couplet in the
poem—are different from the rest not only in sound
effect but also in content. The first twelve lines of the
poem outline a situation or a feeling, but the final couplet
expresses some comment on it. This final comment
'clinches' the whole sonnet and gives it a finality which
would be less effective if it were not for the sound effect
of the only rhyming couplet of the whole poem.

There was a time when rhyme was regarded as almost
an essential feature of poetry, and many people still
believe that unless a poem contains a regular system of
rhyme it is not true poetry. This attitude must be rejected.
In modern poetry especially—but not exclusively in
modern poetry—we have come to see that the use of
rhyme can be very valuable in drawing attention to
something important but that it is not an essential feature
of poetry.

Several different kinds of rhyme can be identified. The
first of these is *full rhyme*—two words where the stressed
vowels are identical in sound, and any consonants which
follow are also identical. Thus 'strength' and 'length',
'flow' and 'throw', 'shut' and 'cut' are full rhymes, but
'stuff' and 'off' are not, since they have different vowel
sounds, and 'note' and 'code' are not since they have
different consonant sounds. We must, of course, be aware
of regional differences of pronunciation. A southern
English poet might intend a full rhyme when he uses

'earth' and 'birth', whereas to many a Scotsman these do not represent full rhyme. To such a Scotsman, 'earth' would rhyme not with 'birth' but with 'berth'.

In the days when full rhyme was regarded as essential to poetry, its function was often to give some kind of regular pattern to the sound of the poem, rather than to concentrate our attention on the special importance to the meaning of the rhyming words. Rhyme of this kind can be a considerable source of pleasure. Children, for example, totally untrained in the appreciation of poetry, always enjoy hearing rhymes and making up their own. The writers of television commercials make full use of this apparently instinctive love which we have for rhyme as something purely pleasurable. The way in which it is used, however, demands great skill, and the pattern of rhymes must always be appropriate to what is being said.

Burns, for example, in 'Tam o' Shanter', uses the perfect rhyme arrangement for his purpose. He writes in rhyming couplets—a a, b b, c c, etc. Thus we have a rhyme complete at the end of every second line—and they are short lines too. The result is that the fast flow of rhyming sounds helps to convey some of the lightness and speed so essential in this humorous narrative poem. The same arrangement could not possibly work for Gray's 'Elegy', a serious reflection on the subject of death. Gray, in fact, adopts a pattern of a b a b. Thus we have to read in groups of four lines—and they are pentameters as distinct from Burns's tetrameters—before we hear the full rhyming effect. With the rhyming sounds being so far apart, the effect is to slow down the apparent pace of the poem, and this is obviously necessary in this case. Generally speaking it could be said that when a regular system of full rhyme is employed, a poem which is essentially light-hearted or fast-moving requires its rhymes to occur close to each other, the couplet being the ideal, whereas a poem which is serious or sad or slow-moving requires a more complex pattern, so that the rhyming does not become too obvious.

Even when a poet writes in regular couplets, however, there are various ways in which the pace of the poem can be slowed down. Browning, for example, uses couplets in 'My Last Duchess'. This is a 'dramatic monologue', representing the actual words spoken by a particular person to a particular listener in a particular situation. Obviously a conversation conducted in regular lines of iambic pentameter, with a strong rhyme completed at the end of every second line, would sound like a very peculiar conversation. Yet Browning's poem sounds completely natural. His solution was to vary the positions of the pauses rather than having them occur always at the end of the line. If every line ended with a pause we should hear the rhymes distinctly. Instead of using such end-stopped lines, Browning makes great use of 'enjambment'—the running of lines together without a pause—so that there is a regular pattern of rhyme running through the poem but it never obtrudes to make the conversation sound unnatural. A short passage will serve to illustrate this:—

> "That's my last Duchess painted on the wall,
> Looking as if she were alive. I call
> That piece a wonder, now; Fra Pandolf's hands
> Worked busily a day, and there she stands.
> Will't please you sit and look at her? I said
> 'Fra Pandolf' by design, for never read
> Strangers like you that pictured countenance,
> The depth and passion of its earnest glance,
> But to myself they turned (since none puts by
> The curtain I have drawn for you but I)
> And seemed as they would ask me, if they durst,
> How such a glance came there;"

First read these lines in a sing-song way, maintaining the rhythm

u x / u x / u x / u x / u x,

ignoring the punctuation, and always pausing at the end of each line. At once the presence of the frequently-recurring rhyme can be heard. Then try reading the lines again, this time in the natural way, pausing only when the sense of the words demands a pause or where there is a mark of punctuation. In this reading, the presence of rhyme should pass almost—but not quite—unnoticed. In this way Browning is able to retain the accepted convention of the regular form, but at the same time to write in a language which really sounds conversational.

In the twentieth century many poets have taken this a stage further by abandoning rhyme as a frequently-recurring element of their poetry and using it all the more effectively when for once a rhyme occurs in a position of strong emphasis in an otherwise unrhymed poem. Mention has already been made of Eliot's 'And three trees on the low sky', and we have seen how the three trees seem to stand out from the poem because of the stresses used, but also because of the partial rhyme occurring in the middle of an unrhymed poem. There is another good example in the same poet's 'The Love Song of J. Alfred Prufrock'. This is not a poem without rhyme. Rhymes are scattered throughout the poem, but not in any regular pattern. Suddenly we come to a couplet:—

"Should I, after tea and cakes and ices,

Have the strength to force the moment to its crisis?"
These lines stand out from their surroundings because of their regular 'jingling' rhythm; they are end-stopped, and this draws our attention to the strong rhyme; then we notice an incongruity between the two rhyming words—'tea and cakes and ices', with all their connotations of triviality, contrasting sharply with the serious connotations of 'crisis'. Here in a nutshell we have the whole poem—a man surrounded by a life of trivialities, who has come face to face with some question of real importance, but who is so conditioned to triviality that he is too timid to say what is really in his mind.

It is in cases like this that rhyme is seen at its best—not mere ornamentation, but a real contribution to our understanding of the poem.

There is one special form of rhyme known as *mid-rhyme*. In a poem based on a regular pattern of rhymes, these rhymes always occur at the ends of the lines. But if the poet needs to add something to the speed of the poem, he can suddenly introduce mid-rhyme—a word in the middle of the line rhyming with the word at the end. The effect is at once to double the apparent speed of the poem. This is a device which Coleridge, for example,

uses frequently in 'The Ancient Mariner'. Sometimes it
is no more than a trick of style, but often it is very effective. One example occurs in the following stanza:—

"With sloping masts and dipping prow,
As who pursued with yell and blow
Still treads the shadow of his foe,
And forward bends his head,
The ship drove fast, loud roared the blast,
And southward ay we fled."

Here Coleridge is describing the speed of a sailing-ship
driven southwards by a gale. After the rather lengthy
simile of the first four lines, we suddenly have the mid-
rhyme in the fifth line, which admirably conveys the
strength of the wind and the resultant uncontrollable
speed of the ship.

Closely connected with mid-rhyme, though strictly
speaking it is not really a matter of rhyme, is the repetition of words within a line to give additional impetus.
Burns, as we have seen, rightly adopts a very fast-moving
rhythm—iambic tetrameter—for 'Tam o' Shanter'. We
have also seen that the effect of speed is increased by his
use of rhyming couplets rather than a more complex
rhyme-scheme. When he comes to the fastest-moving
section of the poem, he requires something more, and this
he finds in the use of repeated words:—

"The piper loud and louder blew,
The dancers quick and quicker flew."

One of the most interesting uses of rhyme is *half-
rhyme*—sounds which are almost, but not quite, true
rhymes. Either the vowel sounds are not identical, or a
stressed syllable is rhymed with an unstressed syllable.
Probably no poet has used half-rhyme more effectively
than Yeats. Consider the opening passage of 'Easter
1916':—

"I have met them at close of day
Coming with vivid faces
From counter or desk among grey
Eighteenth-century houses.
I have passed with a nod of the head
Or polite meaningless words,
Or have lingered awhile and said

Polite meaningless words,
And thought before I had done
Of a mocking tale or a gibe
To please a companion
Around the fire at the club,
Being certain that they and I
But lived where motley is worn:
All changed, changed utterly:
A terrible beauty is born."

Read aloud, this passage sounds almost unrhymed, except for a few echoing sounds. Yet if we examine it closely we find an absolutely regular rhyme-scheme, a b a b, c d c d, etc. There are various ways in which Yeats has played down the effect of his rhyme. For example, he uses enjambment rather than end-stopped lines, so that usually there is no pause after the rhyming sound to give it emphasis. In one case (lines 3-4), not only is there enjambment, but also the sound of 'grey' at the end of line 3 continues on into 'eighteenth-century houses' in line 4, with no perceptible gap between the words. Above all, however, he uses rhymes which are imperfect in some way. 'Day' and 'grey' are full rhymes, but as we have seen 'grey' passes almost unnoticed since it merges with the next line. 'Faces' and 'houses' seem to rhyme only in their consonants, and even then the 'c' of 'faces' has not the same sound as the middle 's' of 'houses'. 'Head' and 'said' are normal full rhyme, but 'words' is then made to rhyme with itself rather than with something different. In the next four lines the rhyme seems to disappear altogether. 'Done' is strongly stressed, yet it is rhymed with the final syllable of 'companion', which is so lightly stressed that all we hear of it is the final consonant. 'Gibe' and 'club' have totally different vowel sounds. Then the stressed 'I' rhymes with the totally unstressed final syllable of 'utterly'. Finally we have 'worn' and 'born'—a full rhyme in some dialects, but probably not quite in Yeat's Irish pronunciation.

The effect of all this is to reduce the impact that the rhyme makes. Had Yeats used regularly recurring full rhymes, especially in a poem consisting of such short lines, the jingling effect would have been quite out of keeping with his subject matter. At the same time, he is writing a poem, not a piece of conversation, and for this reason requires some of the discipline imposed by rhyme as well as the faint echoes of sound which the reader hears. The result is this compromise—rhyme which does not sound like rhyme. This is a device which Yeats often used, especially to suggest a mood of disillusion and dissatisfaction with the world around him. Such a mood is clearly appropriate here, as he describes the emptiness and triviality of Dublin society before the moment which set the whole country alight, the moment of 'terrible beauty'.

Many other poets have found that a mood of disillusion can be best conveyed by the use of half-rhyme. Wilfred Owen's poetry of the First World War is full of cynicism and disillusion, and this is often reflected in the rhymes he employs. We find this, for example, throughout 'Strange Meeting'. The opening lines will suffice as illustration:—

"It seemed that out of battle I escaped
Down some profound dull tunnel, long since scooped
Through granites which titanic wars had groined.
Yet also there encumbered sleepers groaned,
Too fast in thought or death to be bestirred.
Then, as I probed them, one sprang up, and stared
With piteous recognition in fixed eyes,
Lifting distressful hands as if to bless.
And by his smile, I knew that sullen hall,
By his dead smile I knew we stood in Hell."

These lines are actually rhyming couplets, the most fast-flowing metre imaginable, yet the impression given is of something infinitely sadder than what might normally be expressed in rhyming couplets. This impression is gained partly by enjambment, partly by the use of half-rhyme. Throughout the ten lines quoted, there is no case of full rhyme, and an examination of the rest of the poem will show that this is maintained to the end.

Philip Larkin's poem 'Church Going' has already been seen to be a poem of disillusion. Christianity appears to be outmoded—yet Man still seems to require something from the past to hold on to. The poet's ambivalent attitude to the Church is admirably reflected in his choice of form. It has the disciplined and even intricate rhyme-scheme of conventional poetry of the past, yet through the use of enjambment and half-rhyme the rhyme-scheme never obtrudes, and the mood of disillusion predominates. The first stanza can serve to illustrate the pattern that is used:—

> "Once I am sure there's nothing going on
> I step inside, letting the door thud shut.
> Another church: matting, seats, and stone,
> And little books; sprawlings of flowers, cut
> For Sunday, brownish now; some brass and stuff
> Up at the holy end; the small neat organ;
> And a tense, musty, unignorable silence,
> Brewed God knows how long. Hatless, I take off
> My cycle-clips in awkward reverence,"

Here the rhymes are, obviously, on / stone, shut / cut, stuff / off, and silence / reverence. This leaves 'organ' unaccounted for, an apparently odd line. In fact, however, it is not odd—it is intended as a very weak rhyme with 'on' and 'stone' in lines 1 and 3. Some readers may dispute this, and think that something is being made out of nothing. Perhaps an examination of the endings of lines 1, 3, and 6 in each of the stanzas will convince even the most sceptical that Larkin knew what he was about:—

Stanza 1—on / stone / organ
   2—font / don't / meant
   3—do / too / show
   4—come / some / random
   5—week / seek / antique
   6—silt / unspilt / built
   7—is / destinies / serious

Admittedly the vowel sounds are irregular, but the

repetition of the same final consonants is obviously no coincidence. 'Church Going' is, in fact, a perfect demonstration that a poem is a conscious work of art rather than something arrived at accidentally. Every effect is worked for by disciplined effort, everything—even the most humble comma—has something to contribute to the total meaning of the poem. When we apply the principles of Practical Criticism to a poem such as this, not only do we learn more about the poem itself, but also we learn to reject the triviality of much that masquerades as poetry, particularly in the field of contemporary 'pop' poetry.

The last form of rhyme to be discussed in this chapter is that known as *assonance*—the rhyming of vowel sounds only, not the consonants which follow them. Assonance can occur in any position, not only at the end of the line. Thus we may notice coming fairly closely together a group of words such as 'hound', 'flower', 'bout', and 'howl'. Or we may find 'throat', 'comb', 'soul', and 'boast'. If we have any reason to suspect that the choice of these words is deliberate rather than mere coincidence, we can say that the poet is using assonance.

Assonance can be used as a form of onomatopoeia, as in the example already quoted from 'Morte d'Arthur':—

"So strode he back slow to the wounded king."

Here the recurring back vowel helps to convey the unwillingness of Sir Bedivere to return to Arthur, having failed to carry out the command he had been given.

We should not look for assonance, however, at every turn. Many people claim a beauty in the music of vowel sounds when others, equally sensitive to poetry, can find no trace of it. Of its nature, assonance is less obvious than rhyme and alliteration, and it should be commented on only when it stands out clearly and unquestionably from the sounds among which it is placed. Very often, what appears to be assonance is in fact a combination of alliteration and irregularly placed rhymes. For example, 'Prayer Before Birth', by Louis MacNeice, contains the stanza,

"I am not yet born; console me.

I fear that the human race may with tall walls wall me,
 with strong drugs dope me, with wise lies lure me,
  on black racks rack me, in blood-baths roll me."

Undoubtedly these lines contain many strong sound effects, but not much of the effect is due to assonance.

Only when there is no doubt of the frequent use of a particular vowel sound should we seek an explanation of what it is intended to convey. We have this, for example, in Sylvia Plath's poem 'Daddy'. The first stanza of this poem goes as follows:—

"You do not do, you do not do

Any more, black shoe

In which I have lived like a foot

For thirty years, poor and white,

Barely daring to breathe or Achoo."

If we listen to these words we hear unmistakably the sound 'OO'. There seems to be an almost childlike playing with the sound, as we find often in nursery rhymes. Indeed, this poem has much in common with the nursery rhyme—note the title, for example, and 'Achoo' for 'sneeze', and a suggestion of the old woman who lived in a shoe—and didn't know what to do. If, however, this playing with the 'OO' sound seems childlike at first, as the poem goes on we find the sound recurring more and more insistently, usually in a position of great stress. 'You' occurs very often at the end of a line—three times out of the five lines in the last stanza. The horror of the German concentration camps is suggested by the recurrence of 'a Jew' at the end of three separate lines in the seventh stanza. Then we have,

"A man in black with a Meinkampf look

And a love of the rack and the screw.

And I said I do, I do.

So daddy, I'm finally through."

By now the nursery-rhyme quality has gone, and the tone of bitterness and hatred is even audible as we read the last stanza:—

"There's a stake in your fat black heart

And the villagers never liked you.

They are dancing and stamping on you.

They always *knew* it was you.

Daddy, daddy, you bastard, I'm through."

Notice the three successive lines ending in 'you'—a complete sentence in each case, with a full stop at the end. Notice how in the third of these lines we have an additional 'OO' effect—'They always *knew* it was *you*.' Everything seems to lead up to the utter finality of the last line, so shocking in its impact. Without the build-up of the one sound from seemingly innocent beginnings towards this climax, most of the impact of the last line would have been lost.

6 Visual Patterns

In this final very short chapter we shall be concerned with what a poem looks like when it is set down on paper. Normally the appearance of poetry is quite unconnected with its meaning. The only features we normally notice are that the lines tend to begin one below the other, they often begin with a capital letter, and there is a pronounced gap separating the stanzas from each other. But occasionally we come across a poem which has been printed in a very special way, and we realise that the shape has something to do with the meaning.

Lewis Carroll, for example, in 'Alice in Wonderland', has a humorous poem called 'A Long Tale', in which he rejects the normal line divisions and begins at the top in big print, the words following a serpentine path down the page, and the print gradually becoming smaller and smaller until it almost defies the naked eye. What he is doing, of course, is using the shape—that of a mouse's tail—to reinforce the pun intended in the title. The whole thing is, of course, a joke, not serious poetry.

Something rather more important can be seen in 'The Planster's Vision', by John Betjeman:—

> "Cut down that timber! Bells, too many and strong,
>   Pouring their music through the branches bare,
>   From moon-white church-towers down the windy air
> Have pealed the centuries out with Evensong.
> Remove those cottages, a huddled throng!
>   Too many babies have been born in there,
>   Too many coffins, bumping down the stair,
> Carried the old their garden paths along.
>
> I have a Vision of the Future, chum,
>   The workers' flats in fields of soya beans
>   Tower up like silver pencils, score on score:
> And Surging Millions hear the Challenge come
>   From microphones in communal canteens
>   'No Right! No Wrong! All's perfect, evermore'."

The first eight lines deal with what the modern planster

thinks of as the archaic past. The final six lines present the same planster's 'Vision of the Future', in which all homeliness and individuality give way to an inhuman efficiency and uniformity. The differing themes of each section are represented visually by differing methods of setting down the lines. Notice the position at which each line begins, and you will see the two different shapes clearly. Notice also how the rhyming patterns of each section corresponds to the visual pattern. At an earlier point in the book we have already noticed differences in lexis between the two parts of the poem, and even a difference in the use of capital letters. Thus we find that all aspects of the poem—style, sound, and even appearance—are perfectly matched to the subject matter.

Another good example of appearance matching meaning is to be found in 'A Coney Island of Mind', by the American poet Lawrence Ferlinghetti. He is trying to show us how the poet, in his attempt to express beauty, has to expose himself to the public gaze, almost like a circus performer, always walking along a tightrope, where one slip can plunge his work from the heights of beauty to the depths of banality. The comparison of the poet with the acrobat is brought out not only by the actual words used but also by their appearance when set down on paper. A few lines will serve to illustrate:—

"Constantly risking absurdity
                              and death
       whenever he performs
                       above the heads
                                 of his audience
the poet like an acrobat
                    climbs on rime
                          to a high wire of his own making"

In recent years, some poets have developed visual poetry even further, producing pure shapes almost totally divorced from logical content. One example is Edwin Morgan's 'Construction for I. K. Brunel'. In this poem, the great bridge-builder is celebrated by a construction of words in the shape of one of his own constructions. There are two vertical columns of words, printed in block capitals, joined together by a span of four horizontal lines of words, printed in small letters. There is no apparent logical content, but the words are not meaningless. The left-hand column consists of a series of variations of Brunel's Christian name, Isambard—short at first, lengthening in the middle, and becoming short again at the end—suggesting the strength of the construction but also its beauty. Somehow this double quality, of strength and beauty at the same time, is brought out in the line 'I AM IRON BARD'. The words on the right are a series of plays on Brunel's surname— again increasing in length in the middle and tapering off at the end—culminating in 'DOM BRUMMELL', perhaps an allusion to the celebrated Beau Brummell. Each line in the span between the two columns begins with 'great' and ends with 'king', these words arranged one exactly below the other. The other words in the span— words like 'suspension', 'canal', 'railtunnel', 'docks', 'towerpier'—are suggestive of the massive kind of works for which the engineer takes credit. The complete poem has a curious visual beauty of its own, and the more it is examined the more 'meaning' seems to emerge.

Perhaps the ultimate in visual poetry is now being approached by those 'concrete' poets who are deserting the printed page and producing three-dimensional poetry, a kind of verbal sculpture. This is a fascinating idea, but has nothing to do with the purpose of this book.

7 Exercises

A Poem About Poems About Vietnam

The spotlights had you covered (thunder
in the wings). In the combat zones
and in the Circle, darkness. Under
the muzzles of the microphones
you opened fire, and a phalanx
of loudspeakers shook on the wall;
but all your cartridges were blanks
when you were at the Albert Hall.

Lord George Byron cared for Greece,
Auden and Cornford cared for Spain,
confronted bullets and disease
to make their poems' meaning plain;
but you—by what right did you wear
suffering like a service medal,
numbing the nerve that they laid bare,
when you were at the Albert Hall?

The poets of another time—
Owen with a rifle-butt
between the paper and the slime,
Donne quitting Her pillow to cut
a quill—knew that in love and war
dispatches from the front are all.
We believe them, they were there,
when you were at the Albert Hall.

Poet, they whisper in their sleep
louder from underground than all
the mikes that hung upon your lips
when you were at the Albert Hall.

Jon Stallworthy

1. This is about a poet giving a public reading of poems protesting against the war in Vietnam. Notice the contrast between 'the combat zones' and 'the Circle'.

   Examine in detail the words of stanza 1 and discover all the ways in which the poet is compared with the fighting soldiers.

2. Account for the item in brackets in this stanza.

3. What is meant by 'but all your cartridges were blanks'?

4. What is being said about the three poets mentioned at the beginning of stanza 2?

5.   "but you—by what right did you wear
       suffering like a service medal?"

   Examine the grammatical structure of this question, and compare it with the conventional 'But by what right did you wear, etc.'. What difference in tone do you detect?

6. Consider the simile used in these same lines, and discuss all that it implies.

7. In the same way consider and discuss the contrast contained in the metaphor,
   "numbing the nerve that they laid bare".

8. What is implied about the poet Owen by the words
   "   with a rifle-butt
   between the paper and the slime"?

9. (a) What exactly is conveyed by "Donne quitting Her pillow to cut a quill"?
   (b) Why is a capital letter used for 'Her'?
   (c) In what way is Donne similar to Owen, despite the obvious difference in their activities?

10. (a) What proverbial expression are you reminded of in
    "   in love and war
    dispatches from the front are all."?
    (b) What do the lines mean?

11. In the last stanza, what is the effect conveyed by the use of the vocative form of address,
    "Poet, they whisper, etc."?

12. (a) Explain the ambiguity contained in
    "the mikes that hung upon your lips".
    (b) In stanza 1 the word 'microphones' was used, but here 'mikes' is substituted. Is the effect different?

13. Each stanza ends with the same line—"when you were at the Albert Hall." What cumulative effect does this produce?

14. The title is 'A Poem About Poems About Vietnam'. What would be the difference in attitude if the were 'A Poem About A Poem About Vietnam'? What do you gather about Jon Stallworthy's attitude to the modern cult of protest?

Lecture Notes

Wish love were as explicit
As this paper on power and thrust
Given before the Engineering Society,
Heard without misgiving or mistrust.

Taken on trust and understood with ease,
Articulate, the lucid magic backed by proof,
While love, dear love, can't tell the wood from the trees,
Unconcerned with thermodynamics, ranges lonely and
    aloof.

Is there a theory, too, about love's dynamic?
A study of Freud, perhaps, and the old masters?
A pragmatic approach like the talk by this engineer?

Beware, my heart, remember the sinking of the *Titanic*,
The *Comet I* in disintegration, the disasters,
The misfires, the miscalculations, the failure of gear,
Hinting that expert man, like love, is fallible
And still has everything to fear.

John Pudney

1. In what situation have the poet's thoughts arisen?
2. What grammatical feature in the first line is consistent with the title? Is this feature maintained throughout the poem?
3. How attentively did the poet listen to the lecture?
4. What is the 'register' of "this paper . . . . . *Given before* the Engineering Society"?
5. Comment on "the lucid magic backed by proof".
6. What emotive quality is contained in "While love, dear love, ..."?
7. In the second stanza, the poet uses the proverbial expression "can't tell the wood from the trees." How does this contrast with the lecture?
8. (a) What verbal links can you find between stanzas 1 and 2, and between stanzas 2 and 3?
   (b) There is no such link between stanza 3 and the final stanza. What effect does this have?
   (c) Can you perceive, nevertheless, a link of a different sort—one of rhyme?
9. (a) In stanza 4, line 2, we have '*dis*integration, the *dis*asters'. This leads us to the next line, with 'The *mis*fires, the *mis*calculations'. What do

these 'mis-' words refer us to near the start of the poem?

(b) How has the poet's attitude to Science changed in the course of his rumination?

10. What attitude of the poet is conveyed in stanza 3 with
"Is there a theory, too, about love's dynamic?"
(Consider especially the use of the word 'theory'.)

11. What is the effect of the succession of three questions in stanza 3?

12. What in the end do you feel is the poet's attitude to (a) Science
(b) Love?

The Folk Singers

Re-turning time-turned words,
Fitting each weathered song
To a new-grooved harmony,
They pluck slick strings and swing
A sad heart's equilibrium.

Numb passion, pearled in the shy
Shell of a country love
And strung on a frail tune,
Looks sharp now, strikes a pose
Like any rustic new to the bright town.

Their pre-packed take will sell
Ten thousand times: pale love
Rouged for the streets. Humming
Solders all broken hearts. Death's edge
Blunts on the narcotic strumming.

Seamus Heaney

1. The poet is not objecting to genuine traditional folk songs. What is he objecting to?

2. (a) Constrast 'Re-turning' and 'new-grooved' on the one hand with 'time-turned' and 'weathered' on the other.

(b) What connotation is suggested by 'turning' and 'new-grooved'?

(c) What different connotation is suggested by 'time-turned' and 'weathered'?

(d) If you have not already made this clear, show that two different senses of 'turning' are involved.

3. What attitude on the part of the poet is suggested by the word 'slick'?

4. (a) Comment on the sound effect of "They pluck slick strings".
(b) Is this sound effect purely onomatopoeic?

5. Can you identify the set of words to which 'groove', 'slick', 'swing' and' sharp' belong?

6. (a) Comment on the effectiveness and appropriateness of the metaphor contained in
"   pearled in the shy
Shell of a country love
And strung on a frail tune."
(b) How does sound contribute to the effect?

7. What contrast is intended between the first three lines of stanza 2 and the last two lines of the same stanza?

8. (a) What is meant by 'Their pre-packed take'?
(b) What is the effect of the sound of the words, and how is this effect produced?

9. Is there any significance in the line division 'will sell / Ten thousand times'?

10. Explain all that is suggested to you by "pale love rouged for the streets".

11. (a) Do you believe that "Humming solders all broken hearts"?
(b) Does the poet believe it?
(c) Give reasons for your answers.

12. By direct reference to the actual words of the poem, say what are the normal themes of folk music.

13. There is only one full rhyme in this poem, that at very end. How do the words thus emphasised the reveal the poet's attitude to his subject?

14. Now that you have examined the whole poem, do you consider that the title conveys more about the subject of the poem than would be conveyed by the same title in the singular instead of the plural?

Mid-Term Break

I sat all morning in the college sick bay
Counting bells knelling classes to a close.
At two o'clock our neighbours drove me home.

In the porch I met my father crying—
He had always taken funerals in his stride—
And Big Jim Evans saying it was a hard blow.

The baby cooed and laughed and rocked the pram
When I came in, and I was embarrassed
By old men standing up to shake my hand

And tell me they were 'sorry for my trouble',
Whispers informed strangers I was the eldest,
Away at school, as my mother held my hand

In hers and coughed out angry tearless sighs.
At ten o'clock the ambulance arrived
With the corpse, stanched and bandaged by the nurses.

Next morning I went up into the room. Snowdrops
And candles soothed the bedside; I saw him
For the first time in six weeks. Paler now,

Wearing a poppy bruise on his left temple,
He lay in the four foot box as in his cot.
No gaudy scars, the bumper knocked him clear.

A four foot box, a foot for every year.

Seamus Heaney

1. (a) What does the phrase 'Mid-term break' normally mean?

    (b) What other meaning does it have in this poem?

    (c) How successful is the choice of title?

2. Comment on the sound of line 2.

3. Why is there a capital 'B' for Big Jim Evans'?

4. "The baby cooed and laughed and rocked the pram". Comment on the absence of commas.

5. Why was the narrator embarrassed by old men standing up to shake his hand?

6. 'Sorry for my trouble' is not direct speech, as is seen by the use of 'my' rather than 'your'. Why, then, is the expression placed in inverted commas?

7. Why is there no noun after the adjective 'eldest'?

8.   "Coughed out angry tearless sighs"
There is an apparent inconsistency here. How can sighs be angry? How can they be coughed out? Justify the poet's choice of words.

9. (a) Comment on the phrase 'soothed the bedside'.
   (b) In what other ways is this 'soothing' effect produced and contrasted with the violent and sudden death the child suffered?

10. Can you justify the poet's use of *'wearing a poppy bruise'*?

11. Why does the poet use 'box' instead of 'coffin'?

12. (a) Comment on the grammar of the last line.
    (b) How does this line stand out visually from the rest of the poem?
    (c) How does sound contribute to the emphasis placed on this line?
    (d) Why should the line be thus singled out?

The Visitors

They know no more than I would how to stand
with flowers, and being men, sheepishly clutch
them, elbows stiffly bent,
as though a touch
of clothes or hand
would wither up the bloom and kill the scent.
They do not know the odd resilience of flowers.
They wait for wife's or child's visiting hours.

Shot on jets of green the tulips zoom
and weigh their stems across the corridors,
heavy and symmetric as eggs.

The visitors
need so much room
the trolleys brush the flowers or knock their legs.
They hinder the stretcher bearing one whose life
hangs in the balance. Someone else's wife.

Then for a nurse they thin to single file
and let her through to supper as though she rushed
to tend an injury.
Awkward and hushed,
they try a smile
then shift and fidget, stood without dignity
at the beck and call of junior nurse or maid,
shielding their flowers, helpless, almost afraid.

Peter Dale

1. From what situation does the poem spring?

2. What impression are you given of the visitors by the fact that the poem opens with 'They', with no reference to any antecedent?

3. How is the awkwardness and embarrassment of the men brought out in the first stanza?

4. Consider the effect of the first two lines of stanza 2, paying particular attention to the force of the words 'shot', 'jets', 'zoom', and 'weigh'.

5. Is the comparison of tulips to eggs appropriate, or it is utterly incongruous?

6. On a casual reading, the second-last line of stanza 2 might easily be misread. Can you explain in what way? Is this intentional?

7. Comment on the grammar of the last sentence of stanza 2. Whose viewpoint do these words express?

8. What contrast is suggested between the end of stanza 2 and the beginning of stanza 3? Can you suggest a way of accounting for the different behaviour of the men in the two situations?

9. Identify an example of dialect used near the end of the poem.

10. (a) How regular is the pattern of rhyme sounds in this poem?

(b) How noticeable is this pattern when the poem is read through?

(c) Try to reconcile these two features.

11. (a) How do the sound effects of the poem combine to place special emphasis on the last word, 'afraid'?

(b) How important is this word to the total meaning of the poem?

After the Wake

During the midnight prayers, split by crying, I could see,
By a loose corner of the mourning blind, the snow
Ridged in a row of small, white, innocent calvaries
Behind the small Christ, strung silver between tall candles.
They are gone now, the awkward men and their women,
Black and crying sweaty tears. At the door,
Open after them, a thin wind from the fields
Slices the waft of the tea and smoke. I am alone,
Finishing a half-bottle, and look, a little maudlin
In the new, cool dark, at the poor rickle of bones
In the box raised in the corner, with the hill silhouettes
On the blind, and little else but the cold
And the smoking candles and the harmless, silver God.

James McCormack

1. What is a wake? Using the information given in the poem, describe what happens on such an occasion.

2. What do you think is qualified by the adjective expression 'split by crying'?

3. What does the poet mean by 'the mourning blind'?

4. " the snow
   Ridged in a row of small, white, innocent calvaries"
   Using all your knowledge of grammar, lexis, and sound patterns, discuss the techniques by which these words are made striking.

5. What sense can you make of 'the small Christ, strung silver . . .'? What does 'silver' refer to? Why 'strung'? (You may not be able to supply

answers to these questions with any confidence, but some attempt may be profitable.)

6. Comment on the grammar of
    "They are gone now, the awkward men and their women".

7. Why does the poet say 'their women' and not 'their wives'?

8. What is meant by 'sweaty tears'?

9. "   a thin wind from the fields
   Slices the waft of the tea and smoke."
   (a) What does this mean?
   (b) How much is contributed to the meaning by
       (i) choice of words?
       (ii) sound effects?

10. 'Finishing a half-bottle' .... 'a little maudlin'. Do these phrases indicate an irreverent attitude to the occasion?

11. Try to account for all three words in 'new, cool dark'. (Look at the last line before answering.)

12. What do you make of 'the harmless silver God'? Remember that more than one meaning is possible at the same time.

13. What part is played by emotional language in this poem? To what extent is emotion actually present?

Homage to a Government

Next year we are to bring the soldiers home
For lack of money, and it is all right.
Places they guarded, or kept orderly,
Must guard themselves, and keep themselves orderly.
We want the money for ourselves at home
Instead of working. And this is all right.

It's hard to say who wanted it to happen,
But now it's been decided nobody minds.
The places are a long way off, not here,
Which is all right, and from what we hear
The soldiers there only made trouble happen.
Next year we shall be easier in our minds.

Next year we shall be living in a country
That brought its soldiers home for lack of money.
The statues will be standing in the same
Tree-muffled squares, and look nearly the same.
Our children will not know it's a different country.
All we can hope to leave them now is money.

Philip Larkin

1. This poem deals with the policy, for purposes of economy, of withdrawing many British troops stationed abroad. Does the poet approve of this policy? How far should our own views on the policy effect our judgment of the poem?

2. The poet says 'and it is all right', 'And this is all right', and 'Which is all right'. What familiar expression is suggested? What philosophy of life underlies that expression?

3. 'For lack of money' in line 2 is quite different from 'We want the money for ourselves at home' in line 5. Which phrase might be used by supporters of the government's policy?

4. What attitude does the poet impute to the government when he says,

    "Must guard themselves, and keep themselves orderly"?

5. What colloquial feature occurs early in the second stanza? Why?

6. The second stanza seeks to justify the decision, yet this is obviously not the tone of the rest of the poem. Whose viewpoint is being expressed here?

7. Stanzas 2 and 3 are linked by the double use of 'next year'. What different attitudes are concealed under this same phrase?

8. "The statues will be standing in the same
        Tree-muffled squares"
    How would the true meaning of the poem be
    reduced if the poet had referred to houses standing
    in the same squares, or buses running along the
    same streets, or trains running along the same rails,
    or any other such expression?

9. "Our children will not know it's a different
        country."
    Expand the meaning of this line.

10. Explain in detail the pattern that can be observed
    in the endings of the lines of the poem.

11. It might be said that the key word in this poem is
    'money'. Attack or defend this interpretation.

12. Comment on the use of the word 'Homage' in the
    title.

No

And one man said, This man can sing;
Let's listen to him. But the other,
Dirt on his mind, said, No, let's
Queer him. And the first, being weak,
Consented. So the thing came
Nearer him and its breath caused
Him to retch; and none knew why.
But he rested for one long month,
And after began to sing
For gladness. And the thing stood
Letting him for a year, for two;
Then put out its raw hand
And touched him, and the wound took
Over; and the nurses wiped off
The poetry from his charred lips.

                                    R. S. Thomas

1. This is a difficult poem to understand fully. What

do you think it is about? Is it violence, vandalism, philistinism, or what?

2. Without any guidance in the form of questions, consider all that you notice in grammar, lexis, and sound, and try to produce a reasonable statement of what the poem means to you.